ORIGAMI

FOR

KIDS AND ADULTS

OVER

+100

MODELS

MODELS OF ANIMALS, PAPER PLANES, FLOWERS, JEWELRY, CHRISTMAS, HALLOWEEN, AND MORE...

YUJI KOBAYASHI

ISBN : 9798860691230

Content

History of Origami 1

Before we beging 2

Animals

Animal heads ★☆☆ 9

Pig ★☆☆ 10

Bear ★☆☆ 10

Dog ★☆☆ 11

Cat ★☆☆ 11

Ostrich ★☆☆ 12

Whale ★☆☆ 13

Betta fish ★☆☆ 14

Crab ★☆☆ 15

Cicada ★☆☆ 16

Dove ★☆☆ 17

Rabbit ★☆☆ 18

Cute Rabbit ★☆☆ 19

Duck ★☆☆ 20

Duckling ★☆☆ 21

Cat ★☆☆ 22

Dog ★☆☆ 23

Easy Penguin ★☆☆ 24

Seagull ★☆☆ 25

Butterfly ★☆☆ 26

Fox ★☆☆ 27

Monkey ★☆☆ 28

Bat 1 ★★☆ 30

Bat 2 ★★☆ 31

Pig ★★☆ 33

Crab ★★☆ 35

Squirrel ★★☆ 37

Sea Horse ★★☆ 39

Crane ★★☆ 41

Flying Crane ★★☆ 43

2 Turtles ★★☆ 45

Sparrow ★★☆ 47
Platypus ★★☆ 48
Pelican ★★☆ 50
Parakeet ★★☆ 51
Penguin ★★☆ 53
Mouse ★★☆ 55
T-rex ★★☆ 57
Bat 3 ★★★ 60
BabyT-rex ★★★ 62
Horse ★★★ 64
Snail ★★★ 66
Swallow ★★★ 68
Jumping Frog ★★★ 70
Parrot ★★★ 72
Reindeer ★★★ 74
Rhinoceros ★★★ 77
Scorpion ★★★ 80

Jewellery
Diamond Ring ★☆☆ 84
Bracelet ★☆☆ 85

Decor
Winged heart ★☆☆ 86
Heart ★☆☆ 87

Flowers
Cactus ★★☆ 88
Windmill flower ★★☆ 90
Morning glory ★★☆ 91
Iris ★★☆ 93
Water lily ★★☆ 95
Rose ★★☆ 96

Halloween
Pumpkin ★☆☆ 98
Ghost ★☆☆ 99
Frankenstein ★☆☆ 100
Witch ★☆☆ 101
Skull ★★☆ 102
Dracula ★★☆ 103

Games

Paper fortune teller ★☆☆ 105
Crown ★☆☆ 106
Menko/ Ddakji ★☆☆ 107
Windmill ★☆☆ 108
Easy Shuriken ★☆☆ 109
Shuriken ★☆☆ 111

Christmas

Santa hat ★☆☆ 112
Rosette ★☆☆ 114
Elf ★☆☆ 115
Christmas bear ★☆☆ 116
Santa Claus ★☆☆ 117
Candy cane ★☆☆ 119
Christmas tree ★☆☆ 120
Snowman ★★☆ 121
Christmas boot ★★☆ 123

Urban

Glider ★☆☆ 125
Airplane ★☆☆ 126
Simple airplane ★☆☆ 127
Private Jet ★☆☆ 128
Fishing boat ★☆☆ 129
Boat ★☆☆ 130
Small boat ★☆☆ 132
Little boat ★☆☆ 133
Pyramid ★☆☆ 134
Hammer head plane ★★☆ 135
Fighter plane ★★☆ 136
Ferry ★★☆ 138

Pratical

Chip cone ★☆☆ 139
Bookmark ★☆☆ 140
Candy box ★★☆ 141
Box ★★☆ 143
Envelope ★★☆ 144
Fruit basket ★★★ 146

Clothing

The shirt ★☆☆.. 148

Sweater ★☆☆.. 149

Nightgown ★☆☆.. 150

Dress ★☆☆.. 151

Evening dress ★☆☆.. 152

T-shirt ★☆☆.. 153

Summer dress ★★☆.. 154

History of Origami

Origami is the art of folding paper to make three-dimensional shapes and figures. It has a long and interesting history. Even though many people think it comes from Japan, origami actually began in different parts of the world and at different times.

Paper folding started around the first or second century AD in China, where paper was first made. Later on, in the sixth century, it spread to Japan. At first, these paper folds were mostly used in religious events and ceremonies.

In Europe, people also enjoyed folding paper. It was popular in countries like Spain and Germany, where it was used for fun and learning.

In Japan, origami became a real art form with its own special rules and ways. The name "origami" is made from two Japanese words: "ori" (which means fold) and "kami" (which means paper).

During the Heian period (794-1185), only noble people did origami, mainly for special ceremonies. Over time, everyone started doing it and there were even books written to teach how to fold different shapes.

A famous design, the crane, became a symbol of hope and peace, especially after World War II.

In the 20th century, more and more people around the world started to enjoy origami. Artists and clever people, like Akira Yoshizawa and Robert J. Lang, found new ways to fold paper and made origami even more exciting.

Today, millions of people of all ages enjoy origami. It is used in schools, therapy, and even in areas like spacecraft design to solve tricky problems.

Origami is more than just a hobby. It is an art that brings people from different cultures together. It combines beauty and purpose and keeps on amazing and inspiring us. Whether you're a child, a beginner, or someone with experience, origami's story invites you to fold, discover, and find your own way in this time-less art.

Before we begin

To make origami, you'll need a square piece of paper. Traditionally, this would be a 6 inches x 6 inches sheet with one white side and one coloured side.

A single-coloured sheet will work just as well, but it must be perfectly square unless otherwise stated.

In the instructions, the paper will be represented by a square with a grey side symbolising the coloured side and a white side.

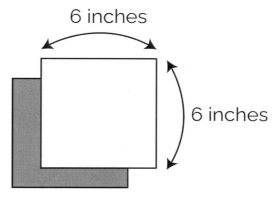

At the top of the page, you'll find information such as: the category, the name of the origami, the difficulty level, and a picture of the finished origami fold.

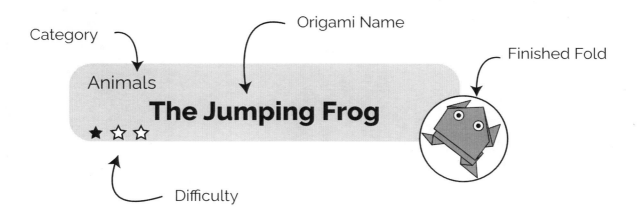

Following this, you'll find diagrams explaining the folding process step by step, marked by numbers and accompanied by explanatory text.

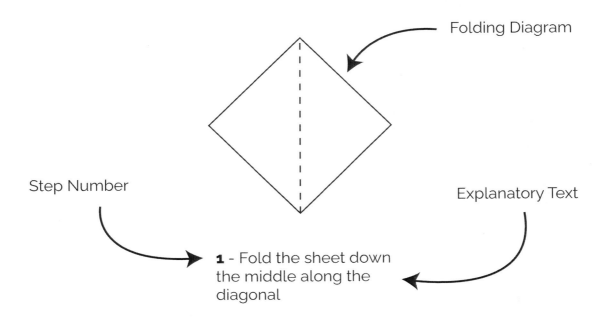

Folding Diagram

Step Number

Explanatory Text

1 - Fold the sheet down the middle along the diagonal

In the diagrams, dotted lines and arrows will guide the folding process. The dotted lines show where to fold, and the arrows indicate the direction of the fold.

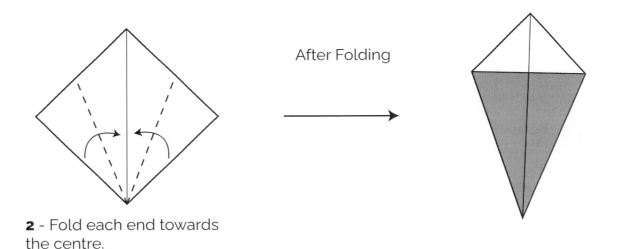

After Folding

2 - Fold each end towards the centre.

As observed in Diagram 2, there's a continuous, thin line in the centre. This line represents the fold marked in the illustration of Step 1.

The circular arrow indicates that you should turn over your origami.

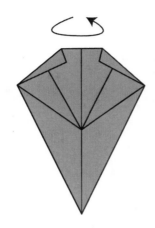

8 -Turn over your origami.

In some instructions, you'll find a scissors symbol, which indicates that a part of your origami needs to be cut.

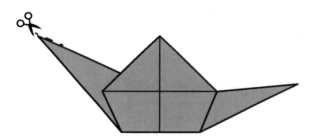

16 - Cut off the tip, only on the top layer.

In all origamis, you'll come across the instruction "mark the fold". A marking fold is a construction fold, similar to a construction line in drawing, that aids the rest of the design. In our case, it makes the remaining folding easier.

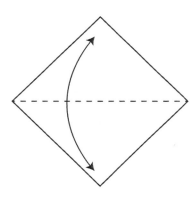

1 - Fold down the middle along the diagonal.

Simply fold the paper along the dotted lines and then unfold it to mark the fold.

Step 1

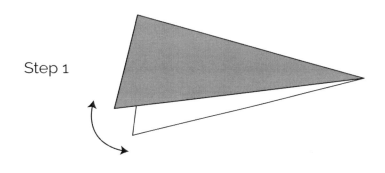

Step 2

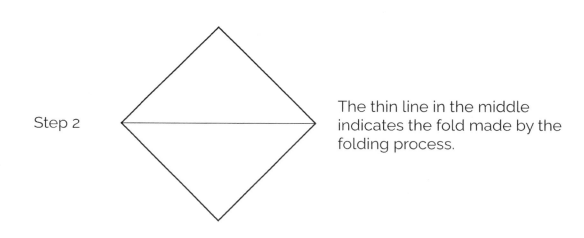

The thin line in the middle indicates the fold made by the folding process.

On some origamis, you'll come across the instruction "reverse the fold". It's easier to first mark the fold along the indicated dotted lines and then reverse the fold.

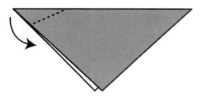

First, mark the fold as shown.

2 - Fold the tip inwards, reversing the fold.

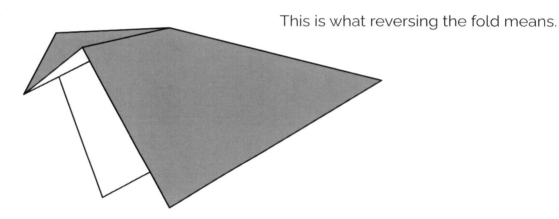

This is what reversing the fold means.

In the instructions, the diagram will be displayed in 2D, not 3D.

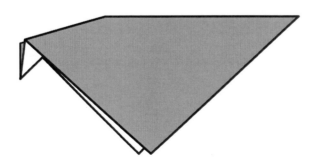

The instruction "fold like an accordion" is technically easy to execute, but difficult to explain. Here's an example:

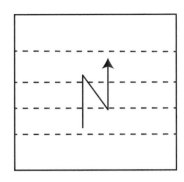

1 - Fold like an accordion, following the dotted lines.

Simply fold your origami in a stair-like manner.

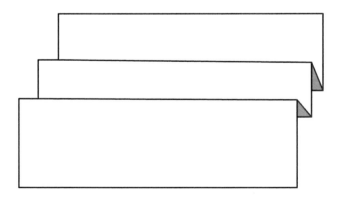

Practical Tips:

Make sure your hands are dry.

Start with simple origamis to get familiar with the paper, as well as the illustrations and instructions.

Use a flat surface to make folding easier, like a table.

Avoid using cardstock sheets if you're a beginner; the thickness makes folding more challenging.

For marking folds, similar to construction lines in drawing, don't press too hard to avoid tearing the sheet.

Don't be afraid to fold your paper; if you're overly cautious about not making holes, your origami won't fold well. It's just paper, and you can shape it as you wish.

When folding your origami, be as precise and neat as possible. Align corners with corners, as this impacts your origami's final result.

Regarding the instructions, focus first on the diagrams; the text is only there if the illustration isn't clear enough. Sometimes, you might need to look at the next step or even the one after to understand the direction.

Animal Heads Basic Folding

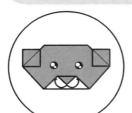  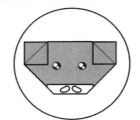 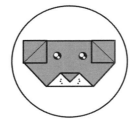

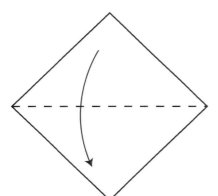

1 - Fold in half

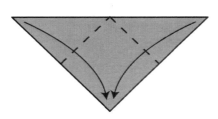

2 - Fold the sides towards the central peak

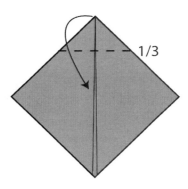

1/3

3 - fold forward to about one-third

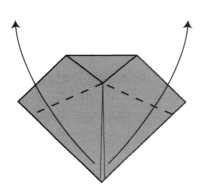

4 - Fold the tips upwards

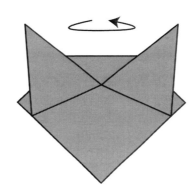

5 - Turn your origami over

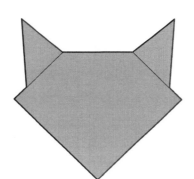

6 - From this origami, you can create 4 different animal heads
-The pig
-The bear
-The dog
-The cat

Pig

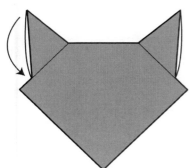

1 - Fold the ears by opening the tips and pressing them towards the center

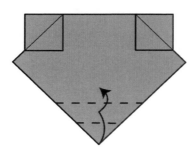

2 - Roll up the tip

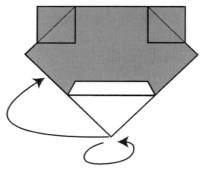

3 - Fold backward and turn over

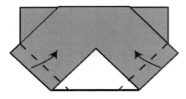

4 - Fold the sides inward

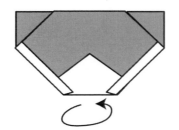

5 - Turn your origami over

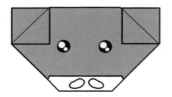

6 - Draw eyes and a snout, and your pig is ready!

Bear

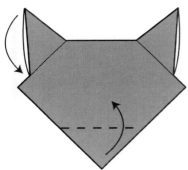

1 - Fold the ears by opening the tips and pressing them towards the center
- Relevez la pointe inférieur
Raise the bottom tip

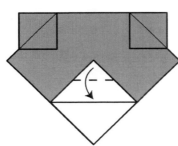

2 - Fold the tip downwards

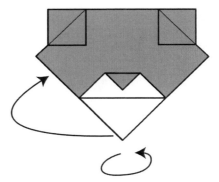

3 - Fold backward and turn over

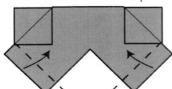

4 - Fold the sides inward

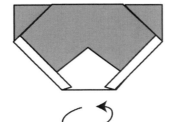

5 - Turn over

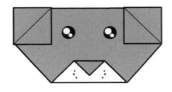

6 -Draw eyes and lips, and your bear is ready!

Dog

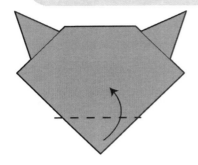

1 - Fold the ears further back
- Raise the tip

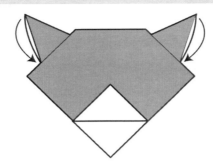

2 - Fold the ears by opening
the tips and crushing
them towards the center

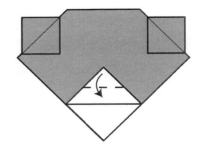

3 - Fold the tip
downwards

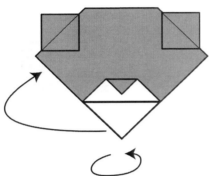

4 - Fold the tip backward
- Turn over

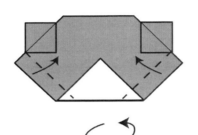

5 - Fold the sides inward
- Turn over

6 - Draw a face,
and your dog is finished!

Cat

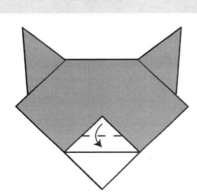

1 - Fold the tip upwards

2 - Fold the tip downwards

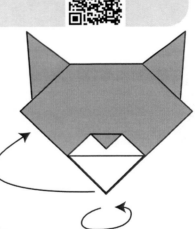

3 - Fold the tip backward
- Turn over

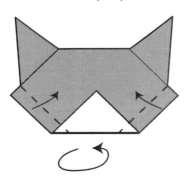

4 - Fold the sides inward
- Turn over

5 - Draw a face,
and your cat is finished!

Ostrich

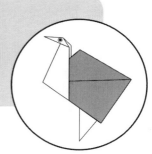

★ ☆ ☆

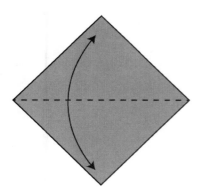

1 - Fold down the middle along the diagonal.

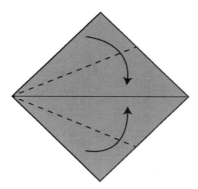

2 - Fold the ends towards the centre.

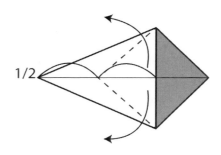

1/2

3 - Fold the ends diagonally outwards.

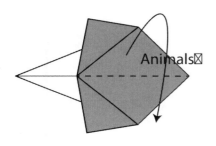

4 - Fold your origami in half.

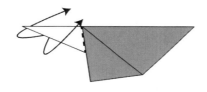

5 - Fold the tip upwards, reversing the fold.

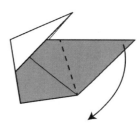

6 - Fold the tip downwards, reversing the fold.

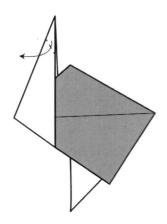

7 - Fold the tip horizontally, reversing the fold.

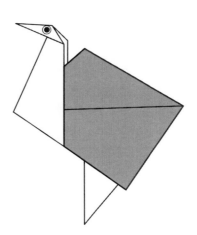

Your ostrich is ready!

Whale

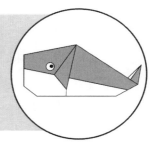

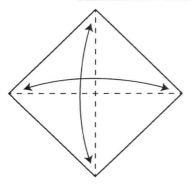

1 - Mark the folds in the centre of the sheet.

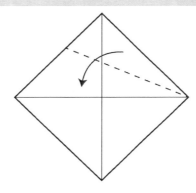

2 - Fold the corner towards the centre.

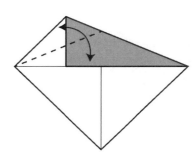

3 - Mark the fold towards the centre of the sheet.

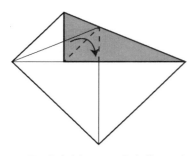

4 - Refold by unfolding the corner.

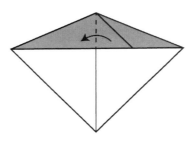

5 - Fold the tip to the other side.

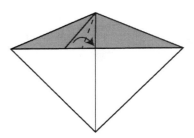

6 - Fold the tip towards the centre.

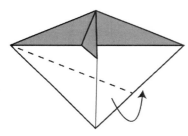

7 - Fold the bottom part to the back.

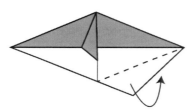

8 - Fold the bottom part to the back again.

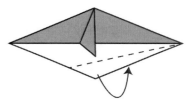

9 - Fold the bottom part to the back once more.

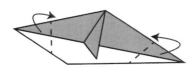

10 - Fold the corners to the back.

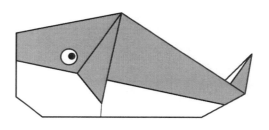

Your whale is ready!

Betta fish

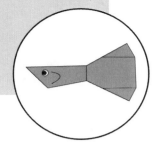

★ ☆ ☆

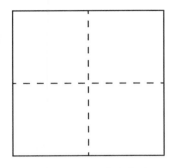

1 - Mark the folds by folding your sheet in half.

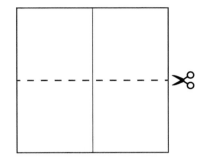

2 - Cut your sheet at one of the construction folds.

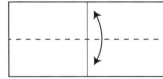

3 - Mark the fold in the centre of the sheet.

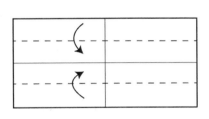

4 - Fold each end towards the centre.

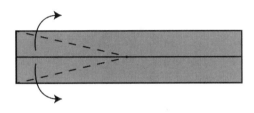

5 - Refold the corners outward, following the dotted lines.

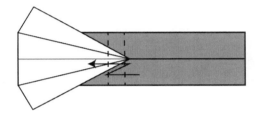

6 - Fold like an accordion along the dotted lines.

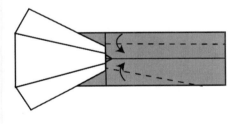

7 - Fold each end towards the centre, following the dotted lines.

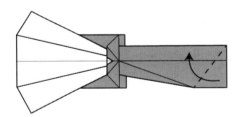

8 - Fold the end diagonally, following the dotted lines.

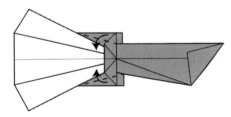

9 - Fold the corners inward, following the dotted lines.

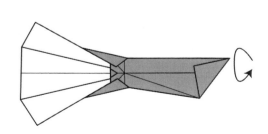

10 - Turn your origami over.

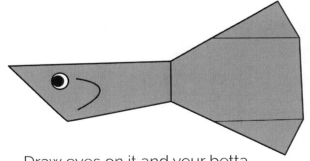

Draw eyes on it and your betta fish is ready!

Crab

★ ☆ ☆

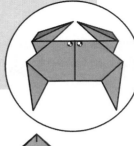

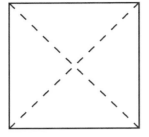

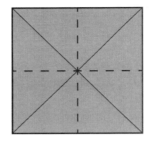

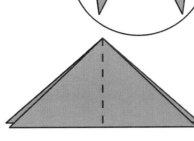

1 - Mark the folds

2 - Turn your sheet over and mark the folds

3 - Press down in the center of the sheet and fold following the marking lines

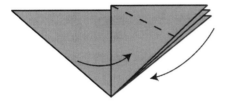

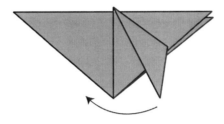

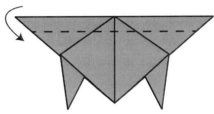

4 - Fold one end over to the other side and fold diagonally to form the back legs

5 - Turn the triangle and do the same for the 2nd leg

6 - Fold the base of the triangle backward

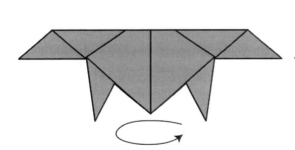

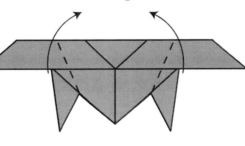

7 - Turn over

8 - Fold the strip and the corner of the body diagonally to form the legs

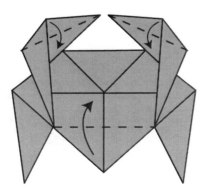

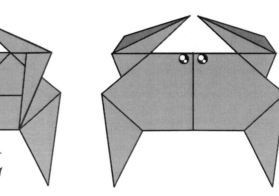

9 - Fold the legs inward diagonally. Fold the bottom part inward. Turn your folding over

10 - You can unfold the pincers to give it some relief. Your crab is finished!

Cicada

★ ☆ ☆

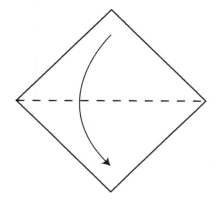

1 - Fold in half

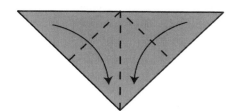

2 - Fold both corners towards the top

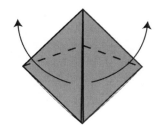

3 - Fold the peaks upward

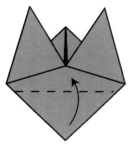

4 - Open it and fold the bottom tip upward

5 - Do it a second time with a slight offset, leaving a space

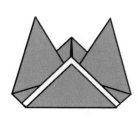

6 - Turn your origami over

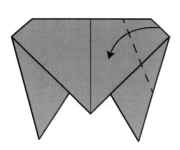

7 - Fold the corner so the white strip is horizontal. Do this on both sides

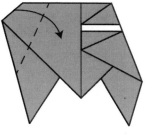

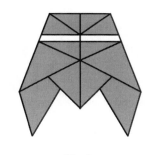

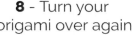

8 - Turn your origami over again

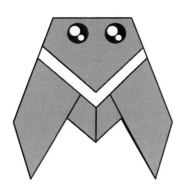

9 - Draw 2 beautiful eyes on it. Now, you have a beautiful cicada

Dove

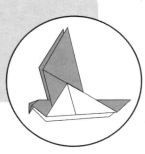

★ ☆ ☆

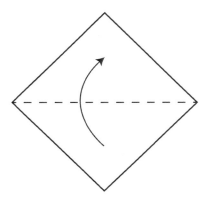

1 - Fold your origami in half diagonally.

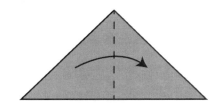

2 - Mark the fold in the centre.

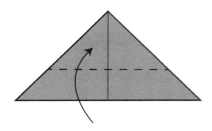

3 - Fold the bottom part upwards, following the dotted lines.

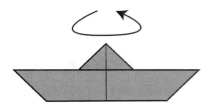

4 - Turn your origami over.

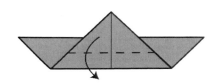

5 - Fold the tip downwards.

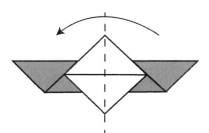

6 - Fold your origami in half.

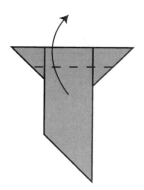

7 - Fold the bottom part upwards on each side to create the wings.

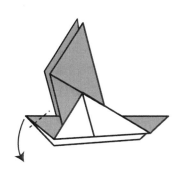

8 - Fold the tip downwards, reversing the fold.

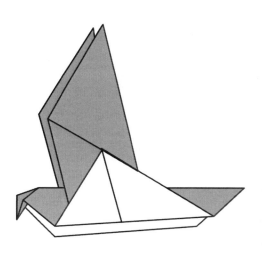

Your dove is ready!

Rabbit

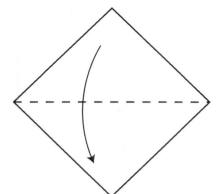

1 - Fold in half

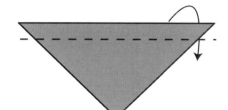

2 - Fold the top part backward

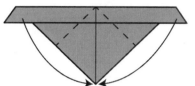

3 - Fold the sides towards the center

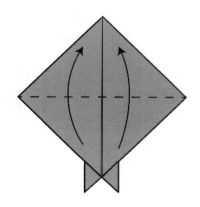

4 - Turn over

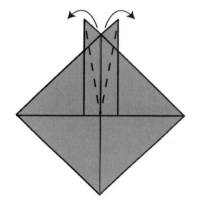

5 - Fold each diagonal inward

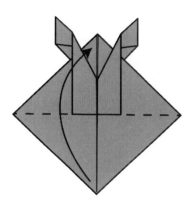

6 - Turn over again

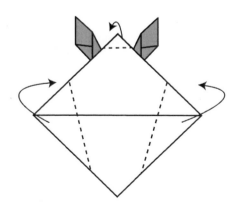

7 - Fold one sheet to the front and one to the back

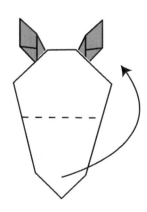

8 - Fold the bottom part backward

9 - Draw a face, and your rabbit is complete

Cute Rabbit

★ ☆ ☆

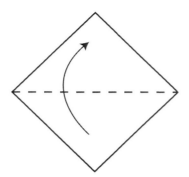

1 - Fold in half
along a diagonal

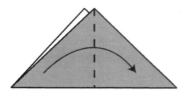

2 - Mark the fold in
the middle of the triangle

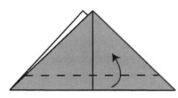

3 - Fold the bottom part

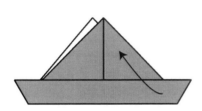

4 - Fold one corner
towards the top

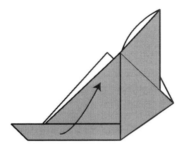

5 - iDo the same with
the second corner

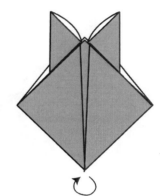

6 - Turn over
your origami

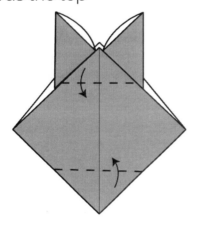

7 - Fold the top
and bottom corners backward

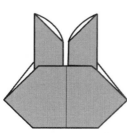

8 - Decorate it to make a cute rabbit   19

Duck

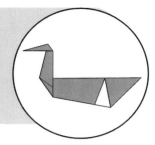

★ ☆ ☆

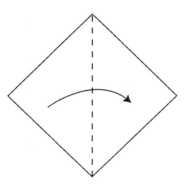

1 - Mark the fold in the centre of the sheet.

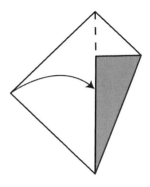

2 - Fold each side towards the centre.

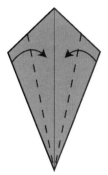

3 - Turn your origami over and fold each side towards the centre.

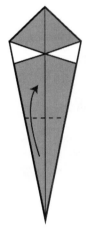

4 - Fold the tip upwards.

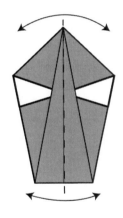

5 - Fold everything in half.

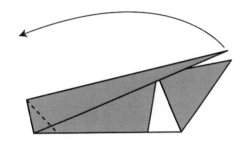

6 - Lift the tip upwards to form the neck.

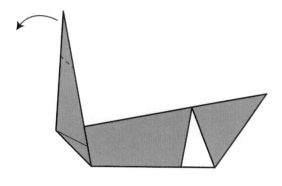

7 - Fold the tip back, reversing the fold.

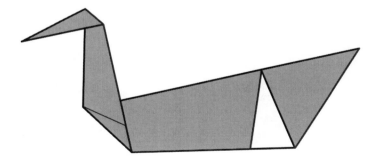

Your duck is ready!

Duckling

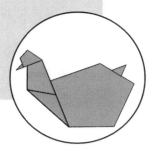

★ ☆ ☆

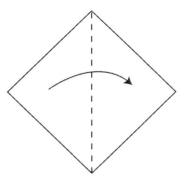

1 - Mark the fold in the middle of the sheet.

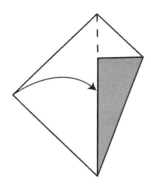

2 - Fold each side towards the centre.

3 - Turn your origami over and fold the tip upwards.

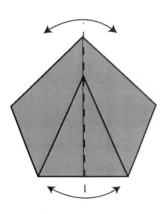

4 - Fold everything in half.

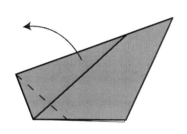

5 - Straighten the tip upwards.

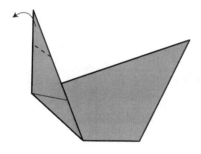

6 - Fold the tip, reversing the fold.

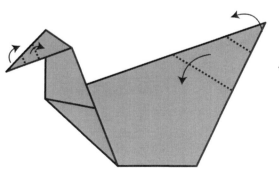

7 - Mark the folds.

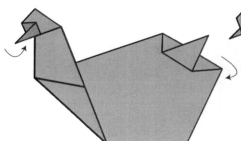

8 - Reverse the folds.

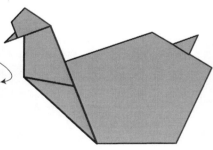

Your duckling is ready!

Cat

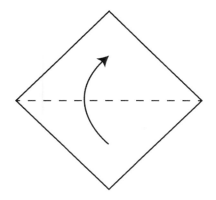

1 - Fold your origami paper in half diagonally.

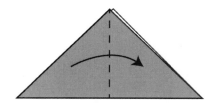

2 - Mark a crease in the middle.

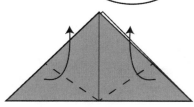

3 - Fold both ends upwards, following the dotted lines.

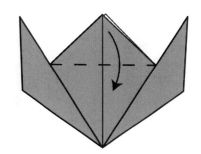

4 - Fold the tip downwards, following the dotted lines.

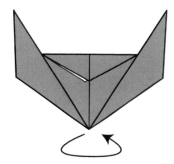

5 - Turn your origami over.

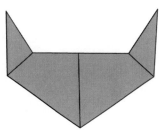

6 - Draw eyes and whiskers on your cat.

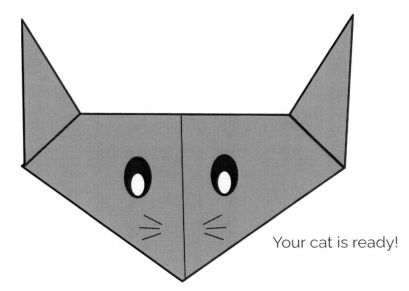

Your cat is ready!

Dog

★ ☆ ☆

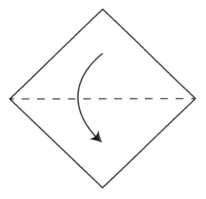

1 - Fold your origami paper in half diagonally.

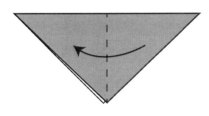

2 - Mark a crease in the middle.

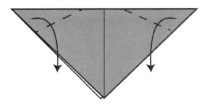

3 - Fold both ends downwards, following the dotted lines.

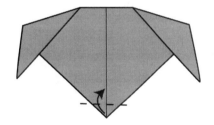

4 - Fold the tip upwards, following the dotted lines.

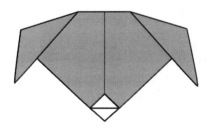

5 - Draw eyes and a nose on your dog.

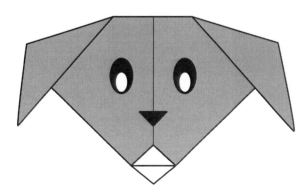

And there you have it, your dog is ready!

Easy Penguin

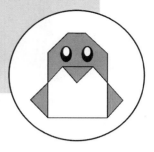

★ ☆ ☆

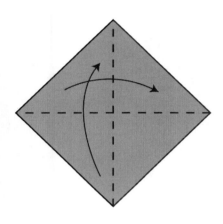

1 - Mark the horizontal folds.

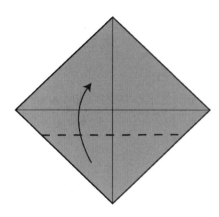

2 - Fold the bottom part upwards following the dotted lines.

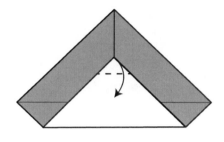

3 - Fold the tip downwards.

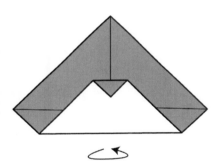

4 - Turn your origami over.

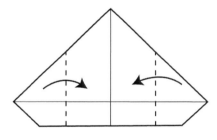

5 - Fold the ends inwards following the dotted lines.

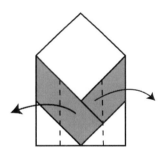

6 - Fold the tips outward to create the feet.

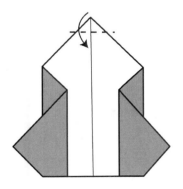

7 - Fold the tips downwards.

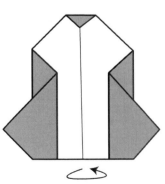

8 - Turn your origami over.

Draw eyes on it and your penguin is done!

Seagull

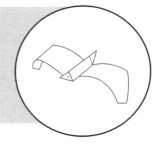

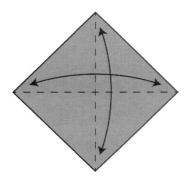

1 - Mark the folds following the dotted lines.

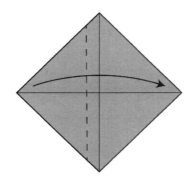

2 - Fold the corner following the dotted lines.

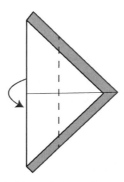

3 - Fold backward following the dotted lines.

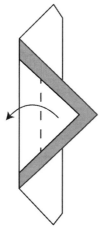

4 - Fold the white peak following the dotted lines.

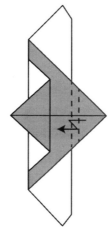

5 - Accordion fold the other peak following the dotted lines.

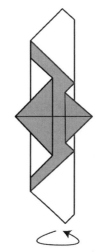

6 - Turn your origami over.

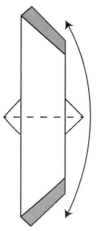

7 - Fold your origami in half.

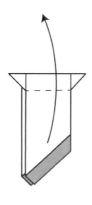

8 - Fold the wings upward.

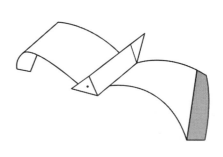

Your seagull is ready!

★ ☆ ☆

Butterfly

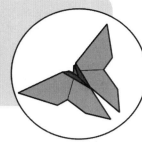

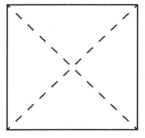

1 - Mark the folds

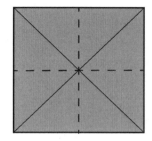

2 - Turn the sheet over and mark the folds

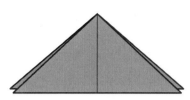

3 - Press on the center and fold the sheet following the construction folds

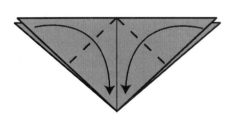

4 - Fold the two corners upwards

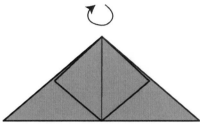

5 - Turn over

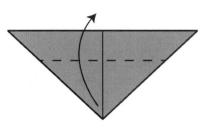

6 - Lift the tip and let it protrude from the base

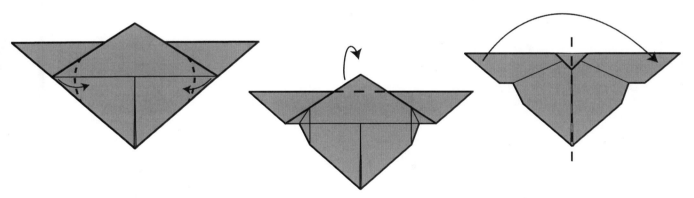

7 - Flatten the corners

8 - Fold the top of the triangle backward

9 - Fold in half

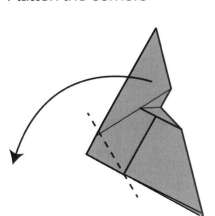

10 - Fold the wings following the dotted lines

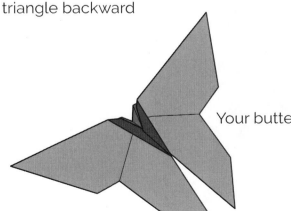

Your butterfly is ready!

Fox

★ ☆ ☆

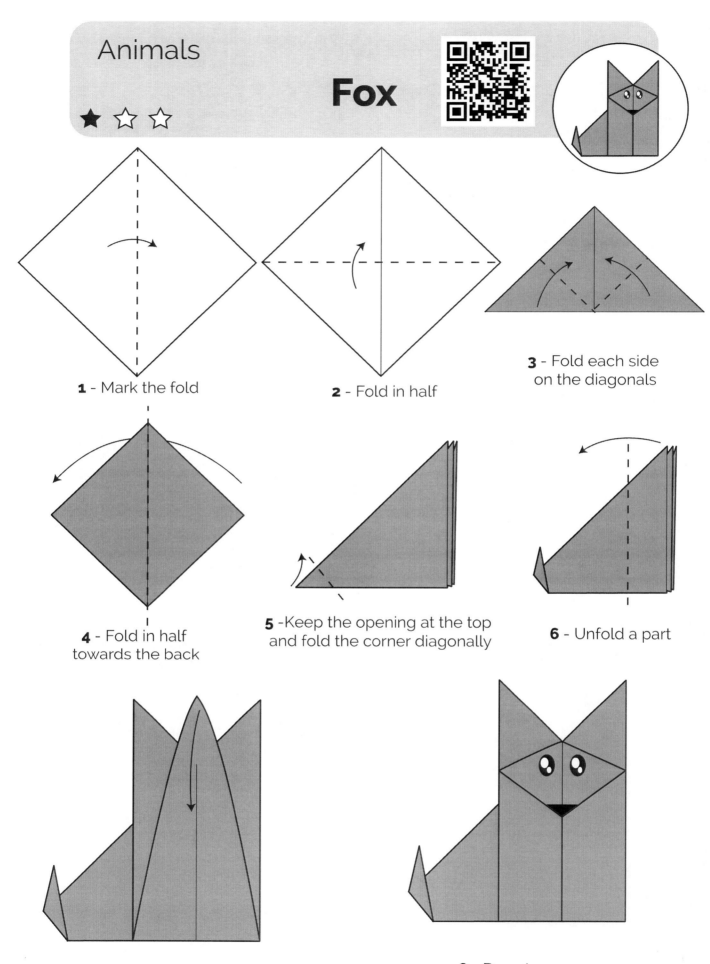

1 - Mark the fold

2 - Fold in half

3 - Fold each side on the diagonals

4 - Fold in half towards the back

5 - Keep the opening at the top and fold the corner diagonally

6 - Unfold a part

7 - Fold down the tip

8 - Draw two eyes and your fox is finished

27

Monkey

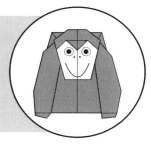

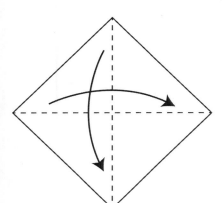

1 - Mark the folds on the diagonals.

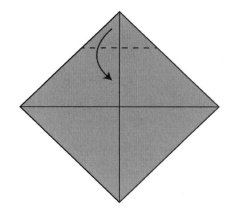

2 - Turn your sheet over and fold the tip following the dotted lines.

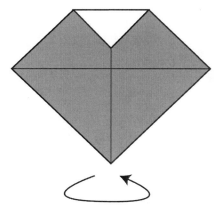

3 - Turn your origami over.

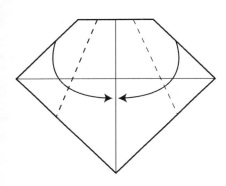

4 - Fold each end to the center fold.

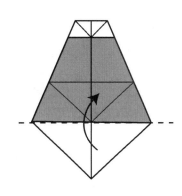

5 - Fold the tip upward.

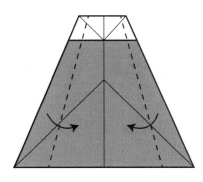

6 - Fold each end towards the center following the dotted lines.

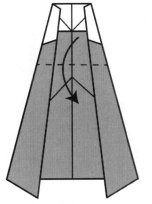

7 - Fold the upper part downward following the dotted lines.

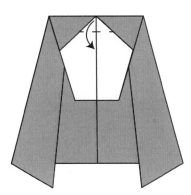

8 - Fold the tip down following the dotted lines.

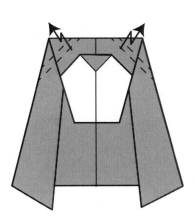

9 - Accordion fold each corner.

10 - Fold the lower parts to create the legs.

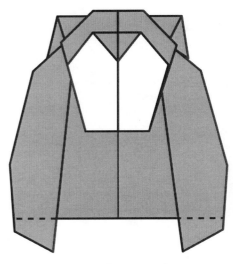

11 - Draw a face on it.

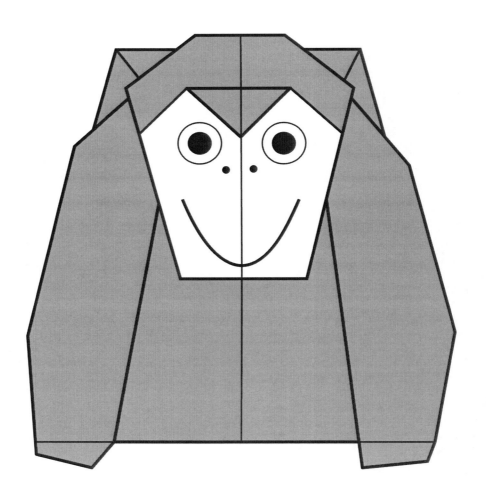

Your monkey is ready!

Bat 1

★ ★ ☆

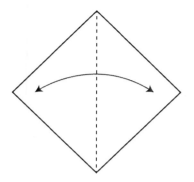

1 - Fold in the center along the diagonal.

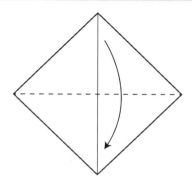

2 - Fold your paper in half along the other diagonal.

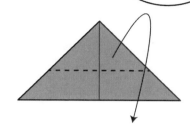

3 - Fold the tip downwards following the dotted lines.

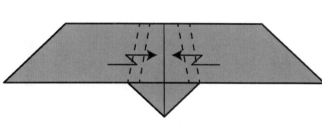

4 - Accordion fold each end.

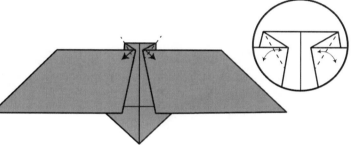

5 - Mark the fold at the dotted lines.

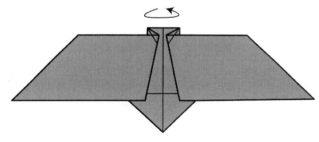

6 - Turn your origami over.

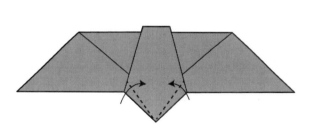

7 - Fold each corner following the diagonals.

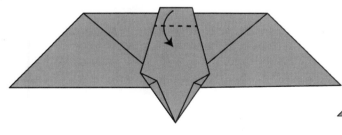

8 - Fold downwards following the dotted lines.

Your bat is ready !

Bat 2

★ ★ ☆

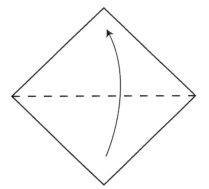

1 - Fold in half

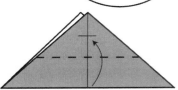

2 - Create a crease in the middle

3 - Fold the base of the triangle to 3/4 of its height

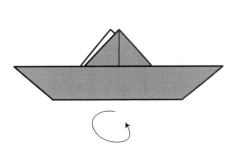

4 - Turn over

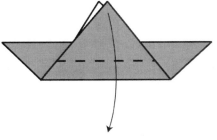

5 - Fold the triangle over half of the bottom part

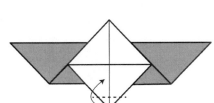

6 - Fold the tip upwards

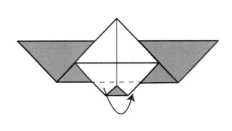

7 - Fold the bottom part to the back to envelop the fold

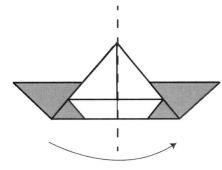

8 - Fold in half

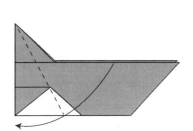

9 - Fold in half diagonally

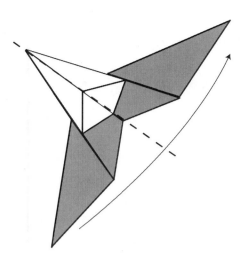

10 - Repeat the process on the other side

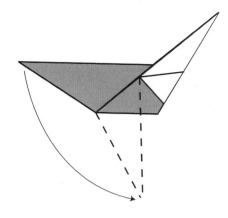

11 - Fold perpendicularly on each side

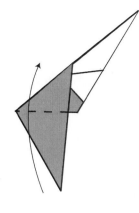

12 - Fold the tips upwards, on both sides

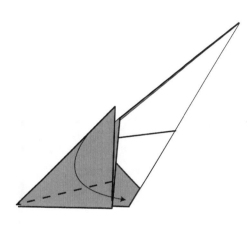

13 -Fold along the diagonal of the bottom part. Repeat on the other side

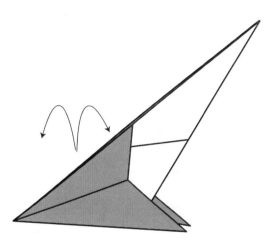

14 - Unfold everything gently

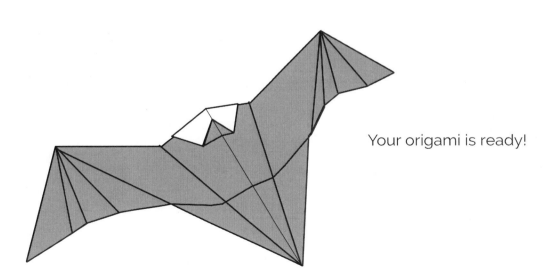

Your origami is ready!

Pig

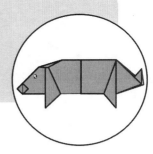

★ ★ ☆

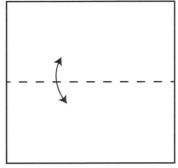

1 - Mark the fold

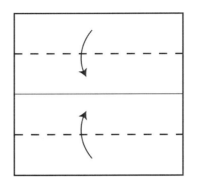

2 - Fold each part in half

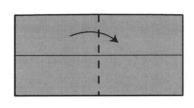

3 - Mark the fold

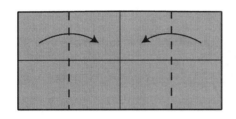

4 - Fold each part in half again

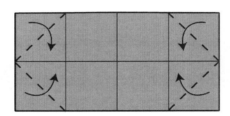

5 - Fold each corner on the diagonals

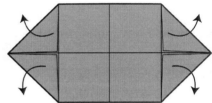

6 - Unfold the corners and reverse the folds

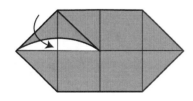

7 - Repeat for each corner

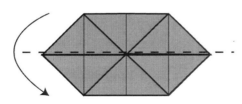

8 - Fold in half

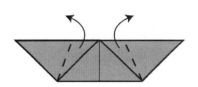

9 - Fold on the diagonals to fold perpendicular

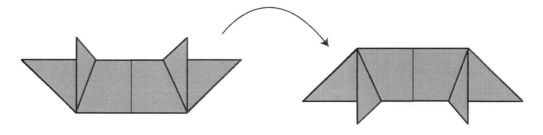

10 - Turn over

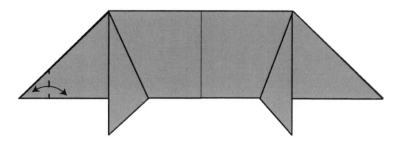

11 - Mark the nose fold and flatten
the nose to form a square

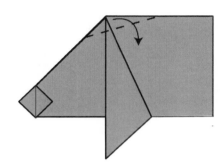 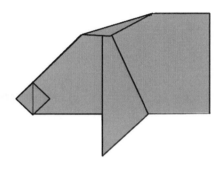

12 - Fold the ears

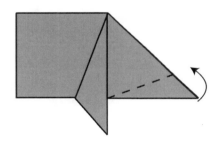 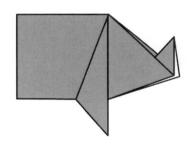

13 - Mark the fold and then reverse the fold inward

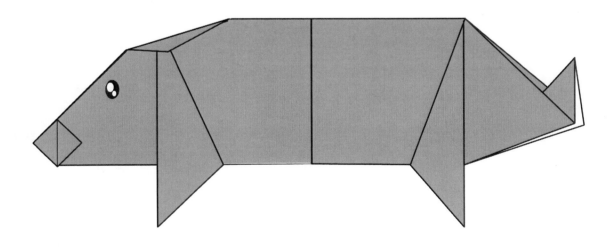

Your pig is finished!

★ ★ ☆

Crab

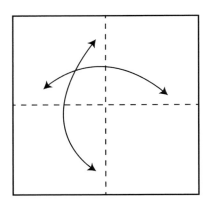

1 - Mark the folds by folding the paper in half in both directions.

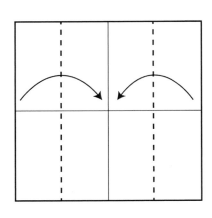

2 - Fold each corner towards the center.

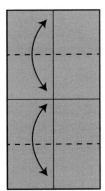

3 - Mark the folds by folding towards the center.

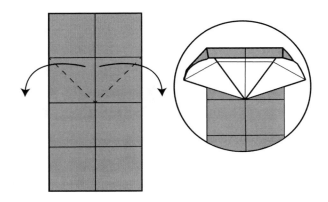

4 - Open your origami at the second square as shown in the diagra

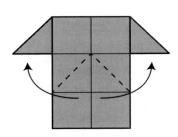

5 - Do the same thing on the other side.

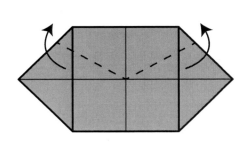

6 - Fold the tips upwards diagonally following the dotted lines.

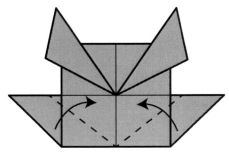

7 - Fold the two other tips in the same diagonal direction following the dotted lines.

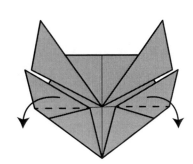

8 - Fold the tips downward to create the legs.

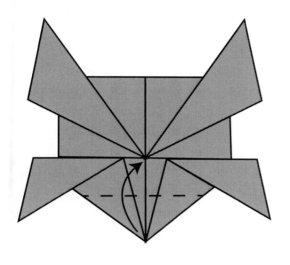

9 - Fold the corner upwards.

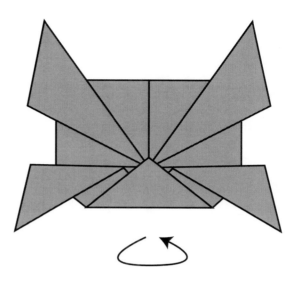

10 - Turn over your origami.

Draw eyes on it, and your
crab is ready !

Squirrel

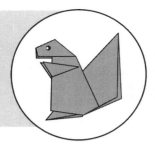

★ ★ ☆

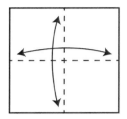

1 - Fold the paper along the center lines.

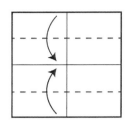

2 - Fold each end towards the center.

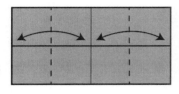

3 - Mark the folds by bending the ends towards the center.

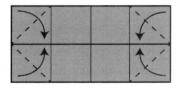

4 - Fold the corners towards the center.

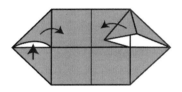

5 - Open and unfold the corner towards the center.

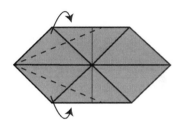

6 - Fold the two ends backward towards the center.

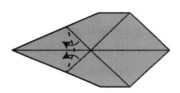

7 - Fold the two tips following the dotted lines.

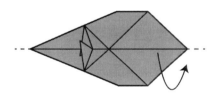

8 - Fold your origami in half.

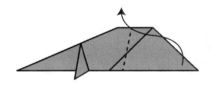

9 - Fold the end by reversing the fold.

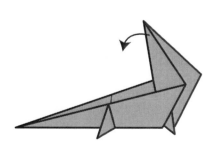

10 - Fold the tip towards the other tip.

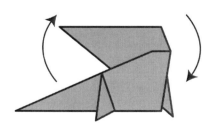

11 - Rotate your origami.

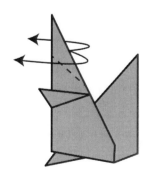

12 - Fold the tip by slightly opening and reversing the fold.

37

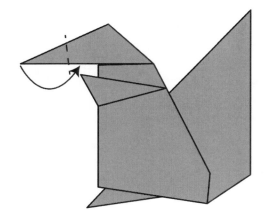

13 - Fold the tip inward.

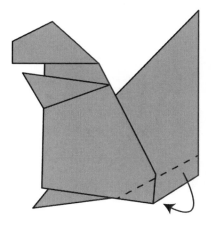

14 - Fold the back inward.

Draw eyes on it, and your squirrel is ready!

Seahorse

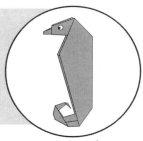

★ ★ ☆

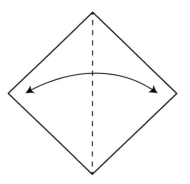

1 - Fold the paper diagonally at the center.

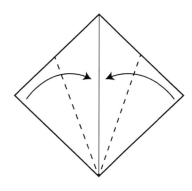

2 - Fold each end towards the center.

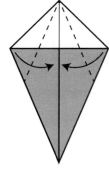

3 - Fold each end again towards the center.

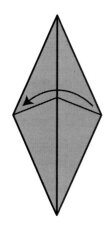

4 - Fold your origami in half.

5 - Fold inward, following the dotted lines.

6 - Mark the fold along the dotted lines.

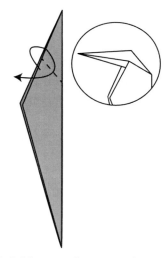

7 - Fold inward, reversing the fold.

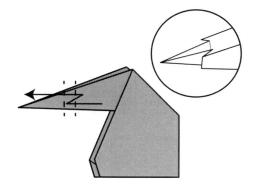

8 - Fold the tip, reversing the fold inward.

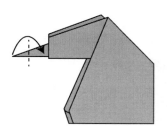

9 - Fold the tip inward again.

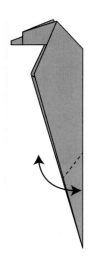

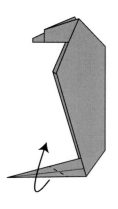

10 - Mark the fold following the dotted lines.

11 - Fold the tip inward.

12 - Fold the tip upwards, reversing the fold.

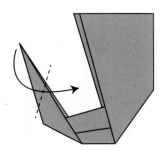

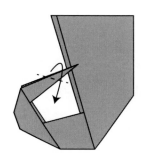

13 - Reverse-fold again.

14 - Reverse-fold once more.

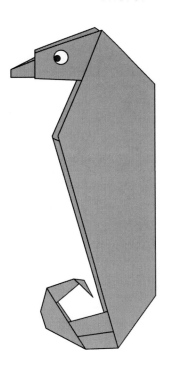

Your seahorse is ready!

★ ★ ☆

Crane

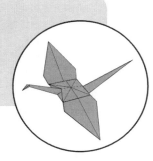

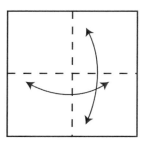

1 - Mark the folds following the dotted lines

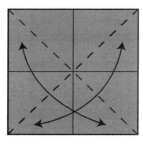

2 - Turn your origami over and mark the folds diagonally

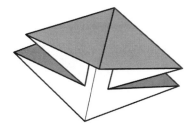

3 - Follow the direction of the construction folds and fold your origami

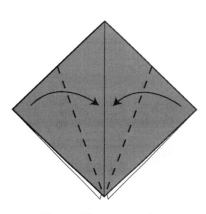

4 - Keep the opening facing down and fold the corners towards the

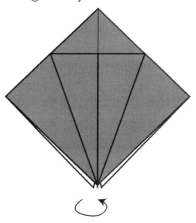

5 - Turn your origami over

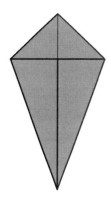

6 - Repeat the folding of step 4

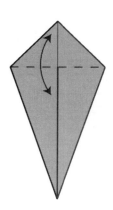

7 - Fold the top corner down following the dotted lines to mark the fold

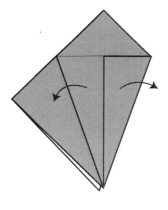

8 - Unfold the corners of both faces

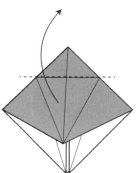
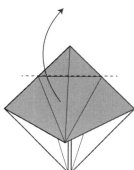

9 - Fold the bottom part upwards by crushing the corners and repeat steps 7, 8, and 9 on the other side

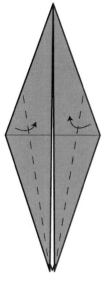

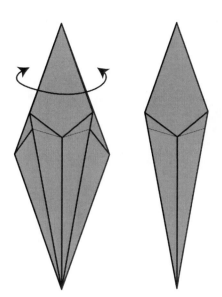

11 - Keep the opening facing down and fold each corner towards the center

12 - Turn your origami over and repeat the process

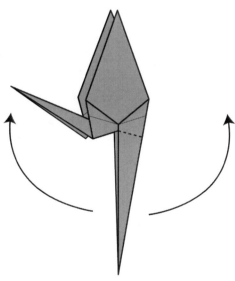

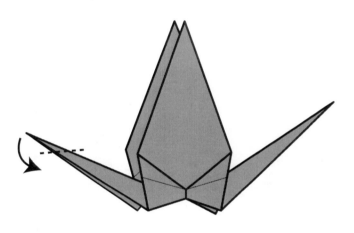

13 - Lift the tips following the dotted lines

14 - Choose one tip and fold it downward to create the head

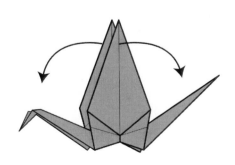

15 - Lower the wings

Your crane is ready to fly!

Flying Crane

★ ★ ☆

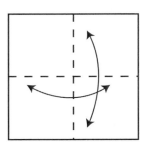

1 - Mark the folds following the dotted lines

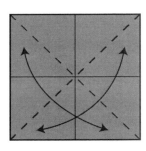

2 - Turn your origami over and mark the folds diagonally

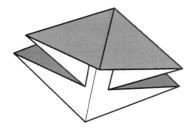

3 - Follow the direction of the construction folds and fold your origami

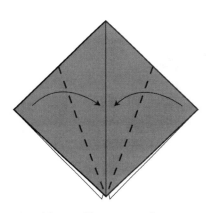

4 - Keep the opening facing down and fold the corners towards the center

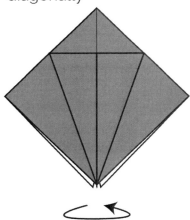

5 - Turn your origami over

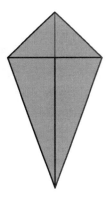

6 - Repeat the folding of step 4

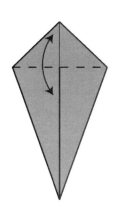

7 - Fold the top corner downwards following the dotted lines to mark the fold

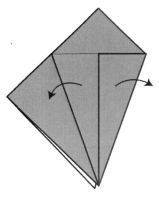

8 - Unfold the corners on both sides

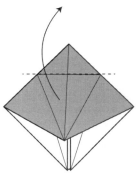
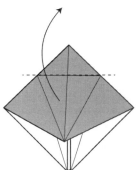

9 - Fold the bottom part upwards, flattening the corners

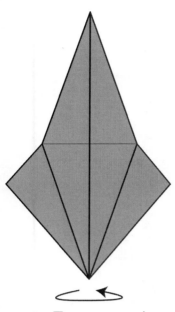

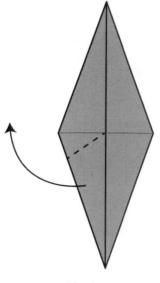

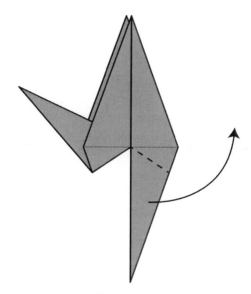

10 - Turn your origami over and repeat steps 7, 8, and 9 on the other side

11 - Lift the tip slightly opening your origami

12 - Do the same thing on the other side

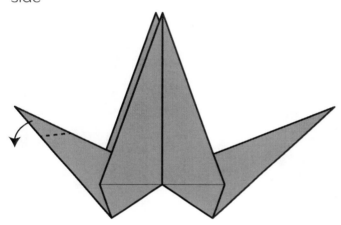

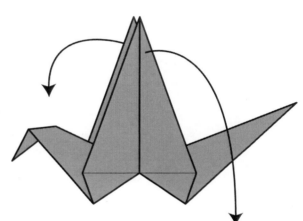

13 - Fold the tip downward and inward to create the head

14 - Fold the wings down without marking a fold

Pull on the tail and your crane will flap its wings!

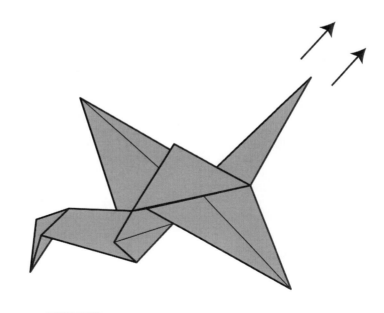

44

The Two Turtles

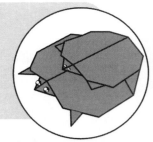

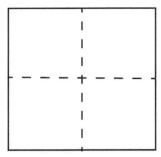

1 - Mark the creases

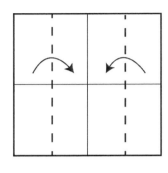

2 - Fold the half-sides

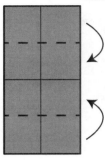

3 - Mark the creases on the halves

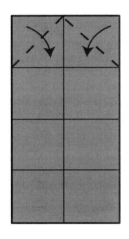

4 - Mark the diagonal creases

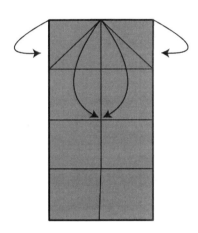

5 - Open the folds and flatten them downwards

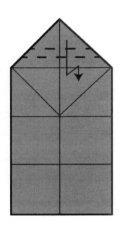

6 - Fold in an accordion style

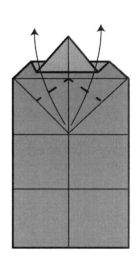

7 - Fold each corner upwards

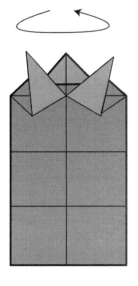

8 - Turn over

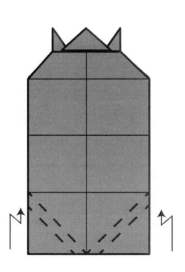

9 - Fold the angles in accordion style

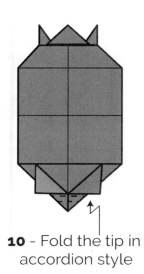

10 - Fold the tip in accordion style

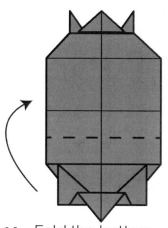

11 - Fold the bottom part upwards

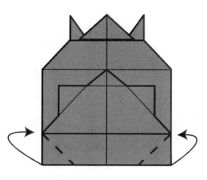

12 - Tuck the corners inside

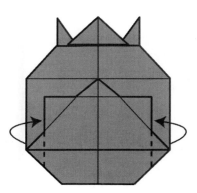

13 - Fold the tips inside

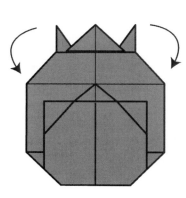

14 - You can adjust the angle of the legs

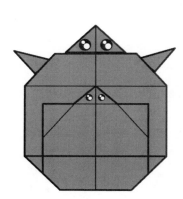

15 - Add eyes

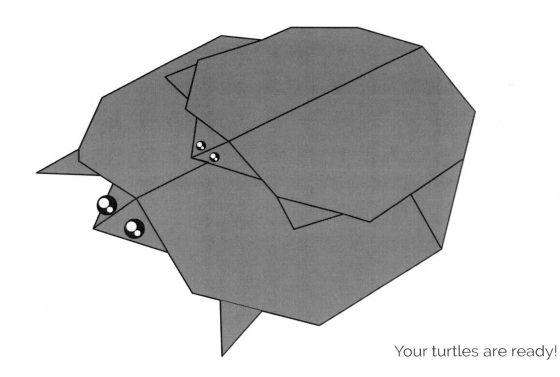

Your turtles are ready!

Sparrow

★ ★ ☆

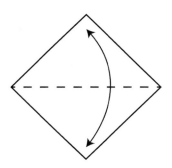
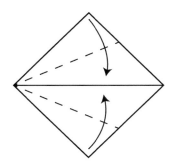
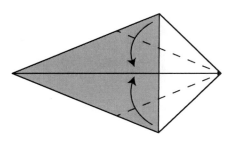

1 - Mark the fold by folding your origami in half along the diagonal

2 - Fold the two corners towards the center

3 - Fold the corners again towards the center

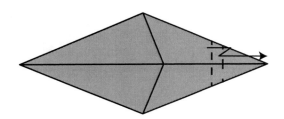
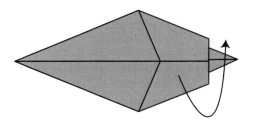

4 - Accordion fold the tip

5 - Fold your origami in half

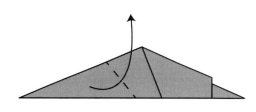
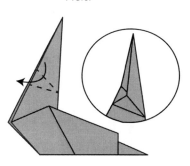

6 - Fold the tip upwards by reversing the fold inward

7 - Fold the tip horizontally by opening the fold

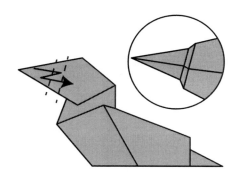
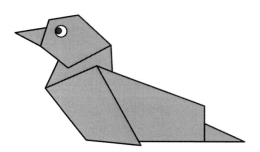

8 - Accordion fold the tip again.

Draw eyes on it and your bird is ready!

Platypus

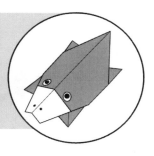

★ ★ ☆

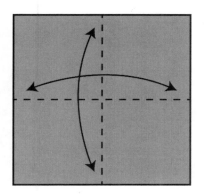

1 - Mark the folds at the center of the sheet

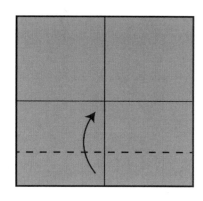

2 - old the bottom part upwards without going all the way to the center

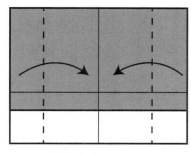

3 - Fold the ends towards the center

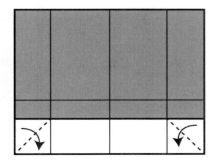

4 - Fold the corners diagonally downwards

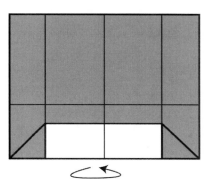

5 - Turn over your origami

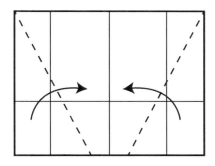

6 - Fold the ends diagonally, following the dotted lines

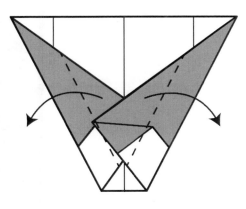

7 - Fold each corner outwards

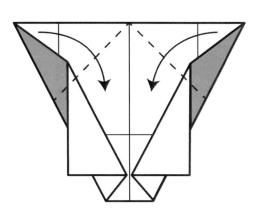

8 - Fold the corners towards the center

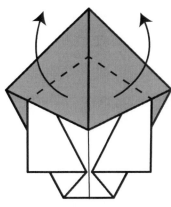

9 - Fold the tips upwards.

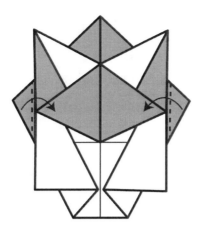

10 - Fold the ends inward

11 - Turn over your origami

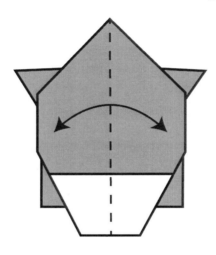

12 - Slightly fold in half

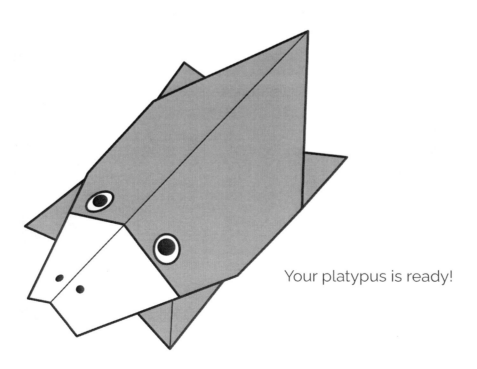

Your platypus is ready!

Pelican

★ ★ ☆

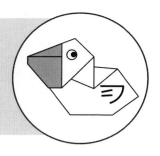

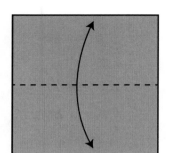

1 - Mark the fold in the center of the sheet

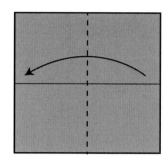

2 - Fold your origami in half

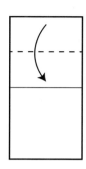

3 - Fold the top part towards the center

4 - Mark the fold following the dotted lines

5 - Unfold your origami upwards

6 - Fold the top part backwards following the dotted lines

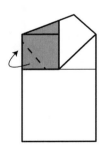

7 - Fold the corner inward

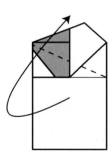

8 - Fold the bottom part backwards following the dotted lines

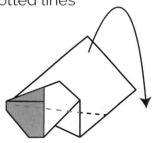

9 - Fold backwards following the dotted lines

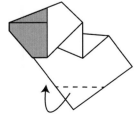

10 - Fold the corner backwards following the dotted lines

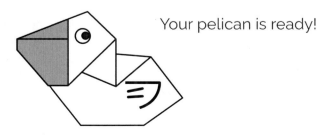

Your pelican is ready!

Parakeet

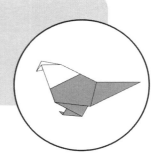

★ ★ ☆

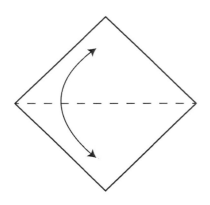

1 - Mark the fold in the center on the diagonal

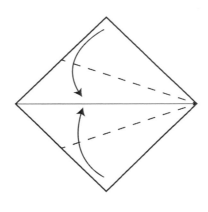

2 - Fold each end towards the center on the previously made marking fold

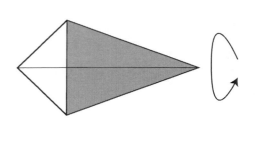

3 - Turn your origami over

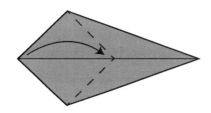

4 - Fold the tip towards the center

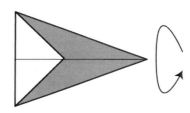

5 - Turn your origami over

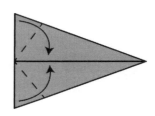

6 - Fold the tips back towards the center

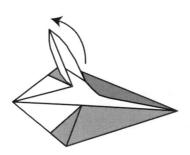

7 - Reopen your origami and reverse the fold outward

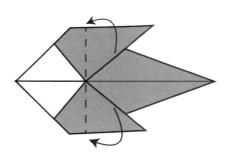

8 - Fold each tip upward following the dotted lines

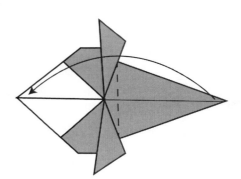

9 - Fold the tail towards the head

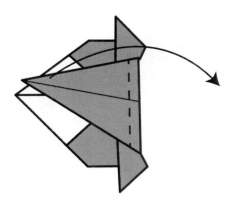 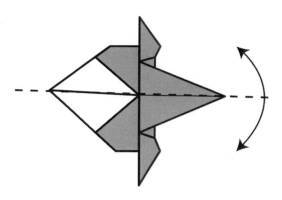

10 - Refold the tail in accordion in the opposite direction

11 - Fold your origami in half

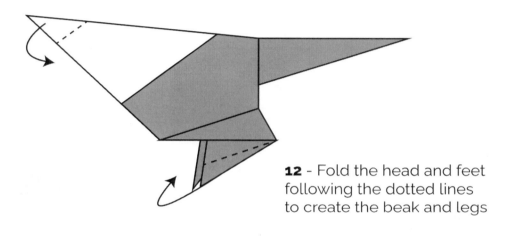

12 - Fold the head and feet following the dotted lines to create the beak and legs

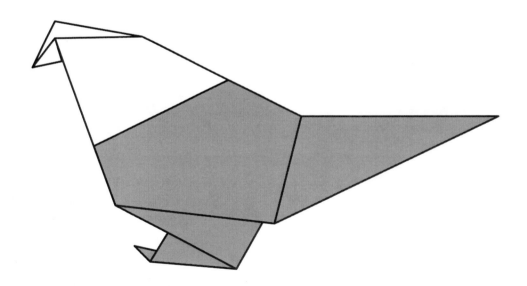

Your bird is ready!

Penguin

★ ★ ☆

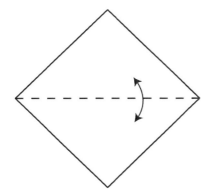

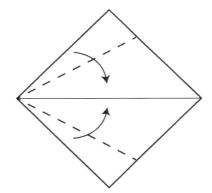

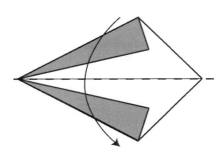

1 - Mark the fold

2 - Fold inward

3 - Fold outward

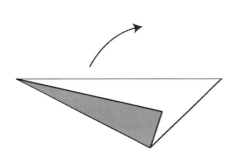

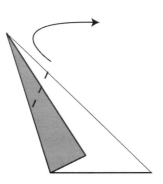

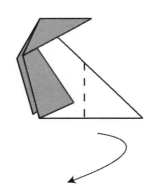

4 - Rotate your origami

5 -Reverse the fold

6 - Reverse the fold

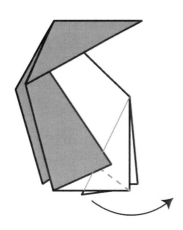

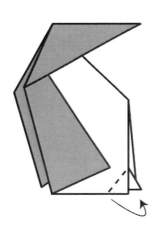

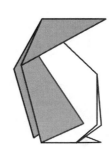

7 - Reverse the internal tip's fold outward

8 - Fold the corners inward

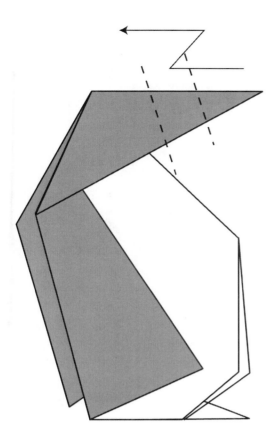

9 - Accordion fold
inward to make the beak

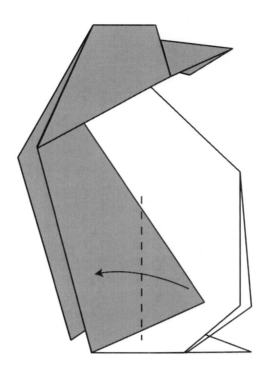

10 - Fold down the tip
to create the wings

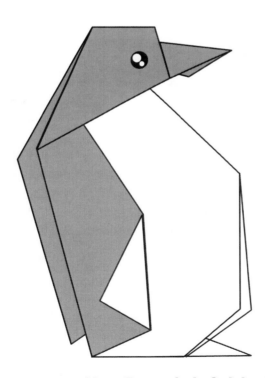

Your Penguin is finished

★ ★ ☆

Mouse

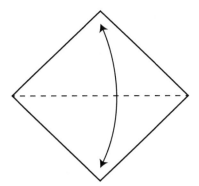

1 - Create a fold in the middle of the paper on the diagonal.

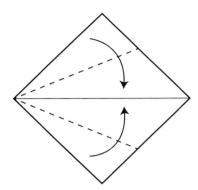

2 - Fold both ends towards the center.

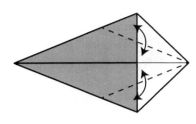

3 - Establish the crease by folding the two ends towards the center.

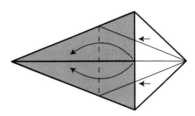

4 - Unfold and fold the corners, following the dotted lines.

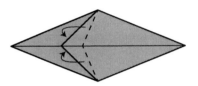

5 - Invert the fold and tuck the two corners inwards.

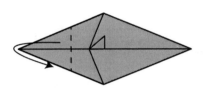

6 - Fold the tip backwards.

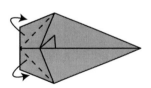

7 - Fold the corners towards the back.

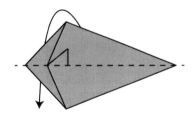

8 - Fold your origami in half.

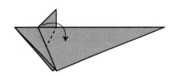

9 - Fold on the other side.

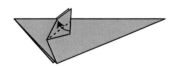

10 - Establish the crease and unfold, reversing the fold.

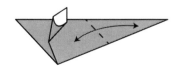

11 - Create the fold.

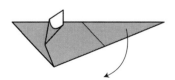

12 - Invert the fold and direct the tip downwards

55

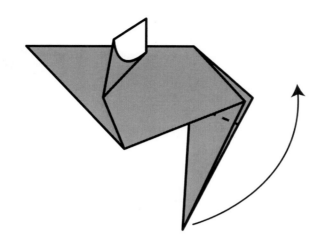

13 - Reverse the fold and point the tip upwards.

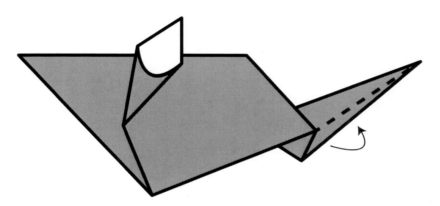

14 - Fold inwards.

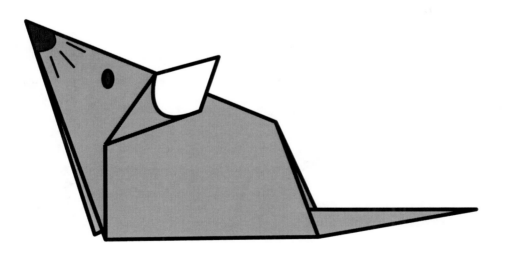

Your mouse is ready!

T-Rex

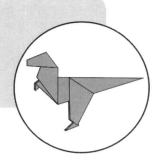

★ ★ ☆

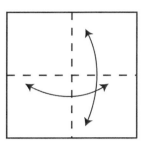

1 - Mark the creases following the dotted lines.

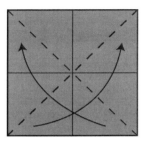

2 - Turn your origami over and create diagonal creases.

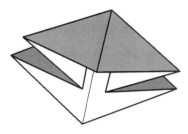

3 - Follow the construction creases and fold your origami.

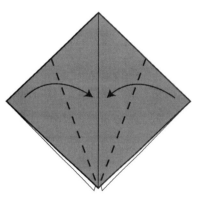

4 - With the opening facing downwards, fold the corners towards the center.

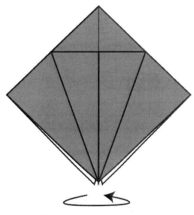

5 - Turn your origami over.

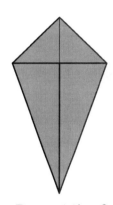

6 - Repeat the fold from step 4.

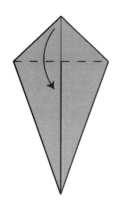

7 - Fold the top corner downwards, following the dotted lines to create a crease.

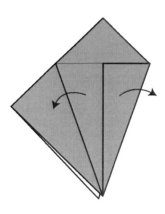

8 - Unfold the corners on both sides.

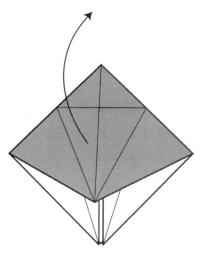

9 - Fold the bottom part upwards and repeat on the other side.

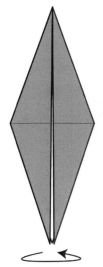

10 - Turn your origami over and repeat the operation on the other side.

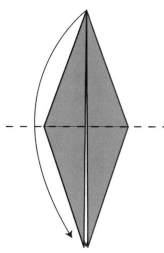

11 - With the opening facing downwards, fold the top corner downwards.

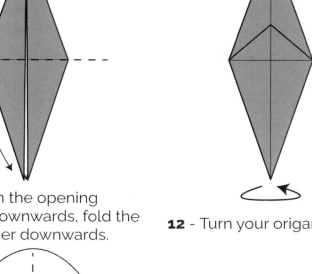

12 - Turn your origami over.

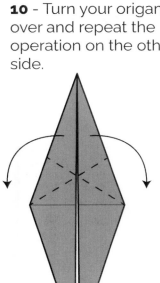

13 - Create creases by folding the tip following the dotted lines.

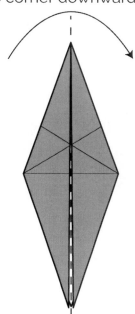

14 - Fold your origami in half.

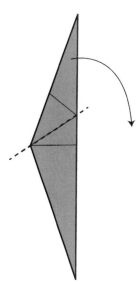

15 - Unfold the crease and reverse the fold following the dotted lines.

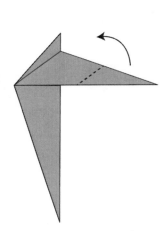

16 - Fold the tip upwards, opening and reversing the fold.

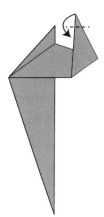

17 - Tuck the tip inside to shape the head.

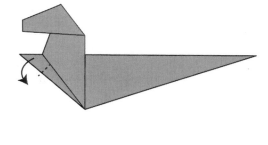

18 - Tuck the tip inside to shape the legs.

58

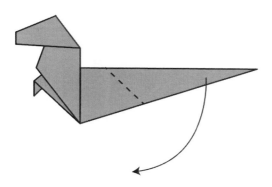

19 - Fold the tip downwards on both sides to shape the rear legs.

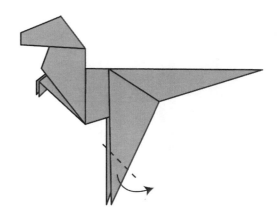

20 - Fold the tip following the dotted lines backwards, reversing the fold, on both legs.

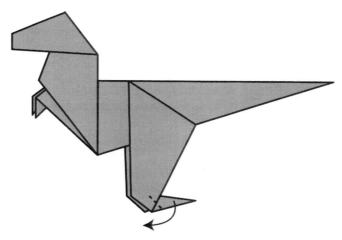

21 - Fold the tip forwards, reversing the fold.

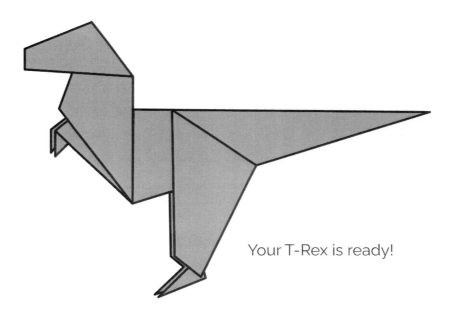

Your T-Rex is ready!

Bat 3

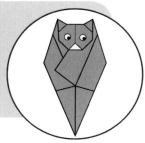

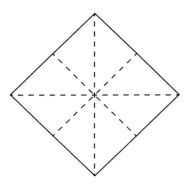

1 - Mark all four creases.

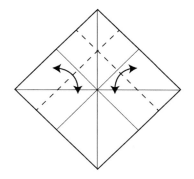

2 - Create the creases by folding the ends towards the center.

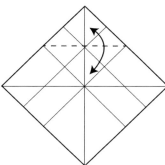

3 - Make a crease by folding the top towards the center.

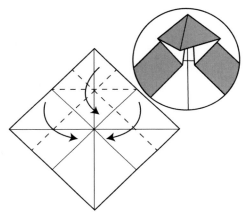

4 - Fold inward following the marked creases.

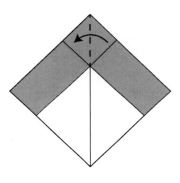

5 - Fold the right corner over to the left.

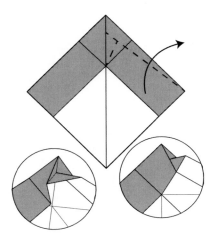

6 - Open and reverse the fold along the dotted lines.

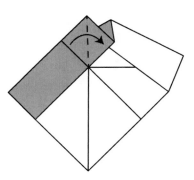

7 - Fold the left corner over to the right and repeat the previous step on this side.

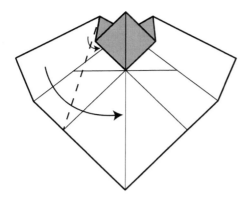

8 - Fold the left wing inwards. The top part should be underneath the head.

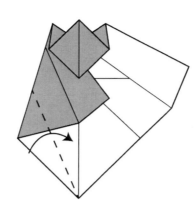

9 - Fold the left corner following the dotted lines.

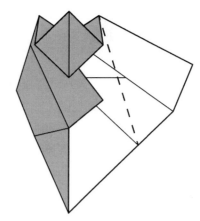

10 - Repeat steps 8 and 9 for the right side.

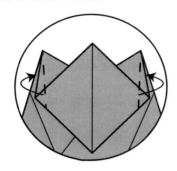

11 - Fold in the cheek areas.

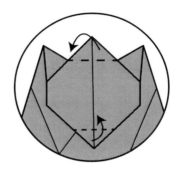

12 - Fold both the top and bottom corners backward.

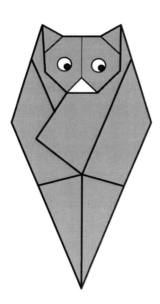

Your bat is ready!

Baby T-rex

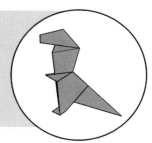

★ ★ ★

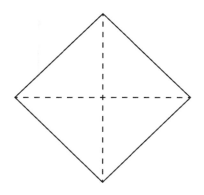

1 - Mark the creases in the center along both diagonals.

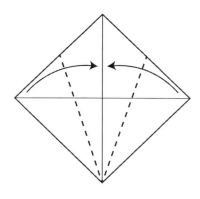

2 - Fold each end towards the center.

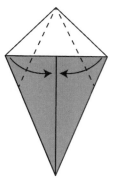

3 - Fold each end again towards the center.

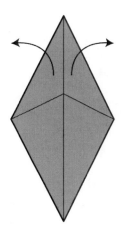

4 - Unfold your origami.

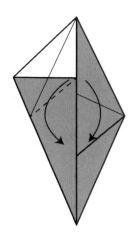

5 - Refold your origami along the dotted lines, folding downwards on each side.

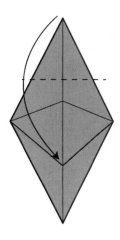

6 - Fold the top towards the corner indicated by the arrow.

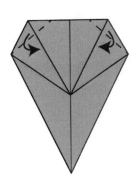

7 - Fold the corners following the dotted lines.

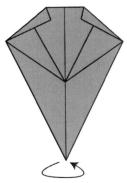

8 - Turn your origami over.

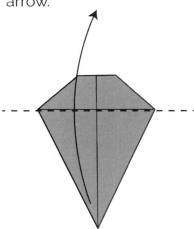

9 - Fold the tip upwards.

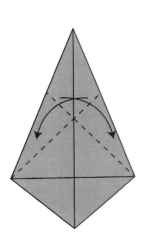

10 - Mark the creases along the diagonals.

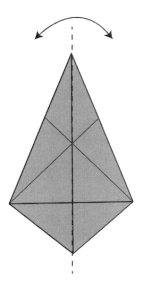

11 - Fold your origami in half by folding the tip following the creases made previously.

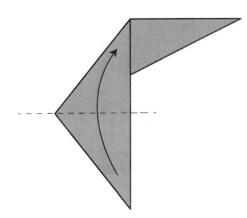

12 - Fold the triangular part upwards on both sides.

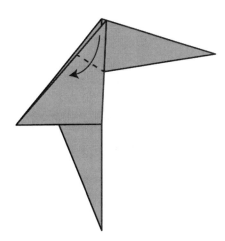

13 - Fold the tip downwards following the dotted lines on both sides.

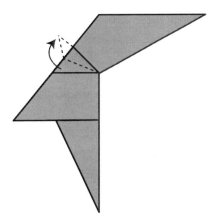

14 - Fold the tip upwards to create the legs.

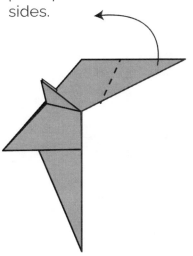

15 - Fold the end by reopening the crease to create the head.

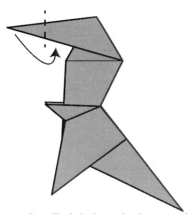

16 - Fold the tip inward.

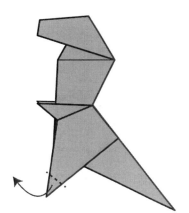

17 - Fold the tip by opening and reversing the creases.

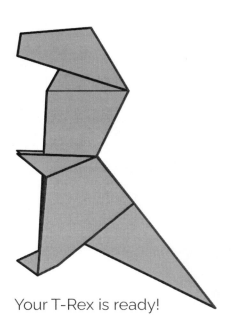

Your T-Rex is ready!

Horse

★ ★ ★

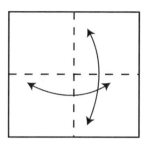

1 - Mark the folds following the dotted lines

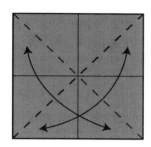

2 - Turn over your origami and mark the diagonal folds

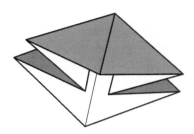

3 - Follow the direction of the construction folds and fold your origami

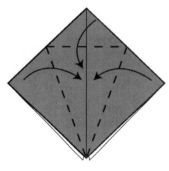

4 - Keep the opening facing down and fold the corners towards the center

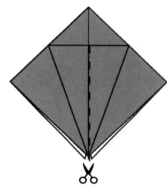

5 - Cut the top sheet

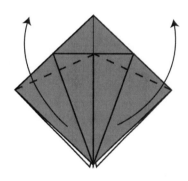

6 - Open upwards

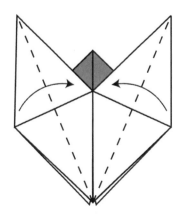

7 - Fold each end towards the center

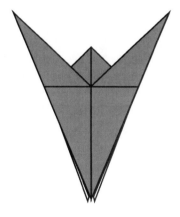

8 - Repeat steps 5, 6, and 7 on the other side

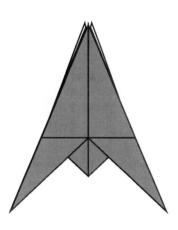

9 - Turn the origami

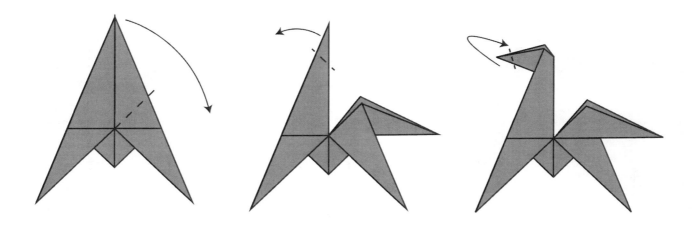

10 - Reverse the fold   **11** - Reverse the fold   **12** - Reverse the fold inwards

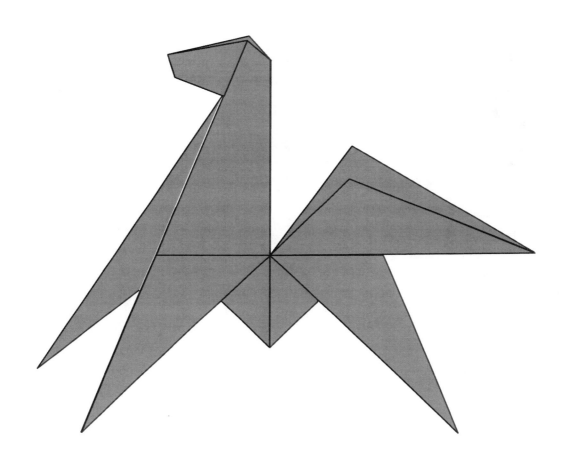

Your horse is finished

Snail

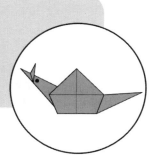

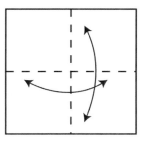

1 - Mark the creases following the dotted lines.

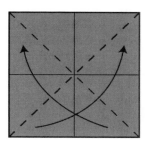

2 - Flip your origami and mark the diagonal creases.

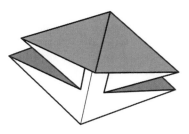

3 - Follow the construction folds direction and fold your origami.

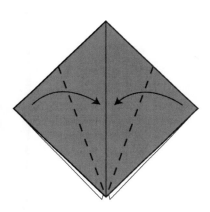

4 - Keep the opening facing down and fold the corners towards the center.

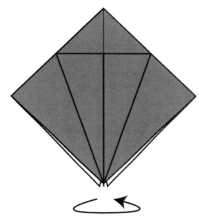

5 - Flip your origami.

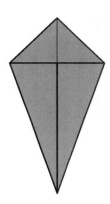

6 - Repeat the fold from step 4.

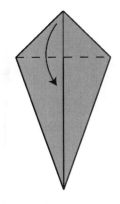

7 - Fold the top corner down following the dotted lines to mark the fold.

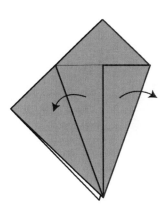

8 - Unfold the corners on both sides.

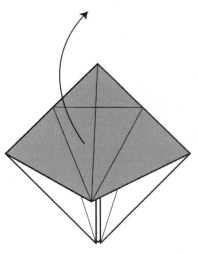

9 - Fold the bottom part upwards. Repeat the process on both sides.

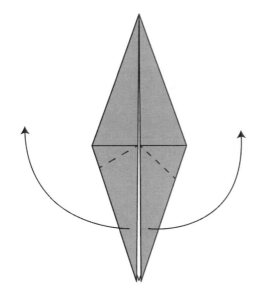

11 - Keep the opening facing down and fold each tip upwards.

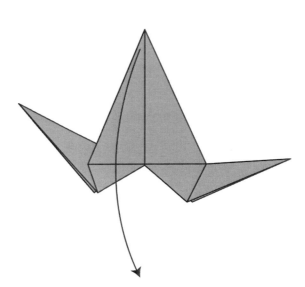

12 - Fold down the top corners on both sides.

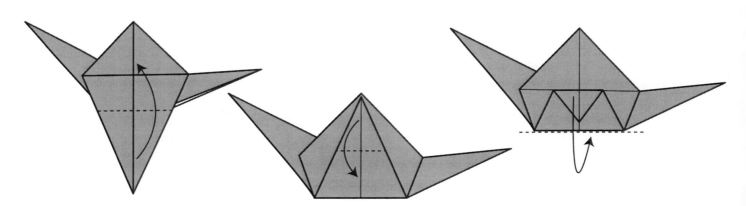

13 - Lift the tips following the dotted lines on each side.

14 - Fold the tip downwards following the dotted lines on both sides.

15 - Fold everything inwards.

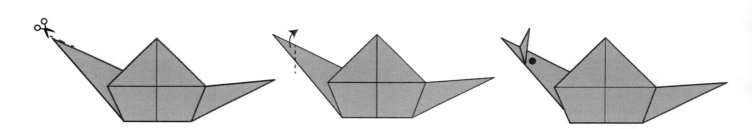

16 - Cut the tip, only on the upper layer.

17 - Fold the previously cut tip upwards.

Your snail is ready!

Swallow

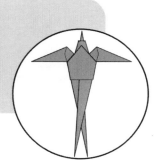

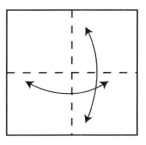

1 - Make the creases following the dotted lines.

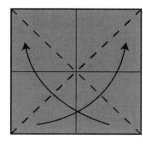

2 - Turn over your origami and make diagonal creases.

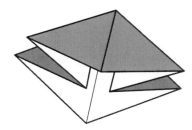

3 - Follow the direction of the construction creases and fold your origami.

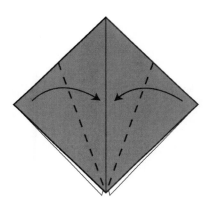

4 - Keep the opening facing down and fold the corners towards the center.

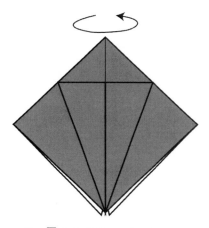

5 - Turn over your origami.

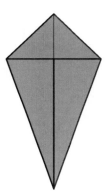

6 - Repeat the folding of step 4.

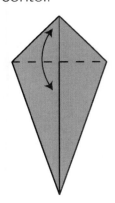

7 - Fold the top corner downwards following the dotted lines to mark the crease.

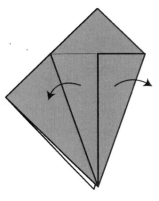

8 - Unfold the corners on both sides.

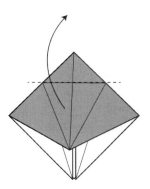

9 - Fold the bottom part upwards, flattening the corners, and repeat steps 7, 8, and 9 on the other side.

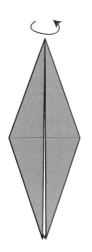

10 - Turn over your origami and repeat the operation on the other side

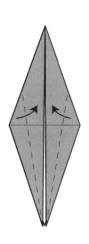

11 - Keep the opening facing down and fold each corner towards the center

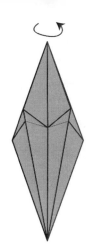

12 - Turn over your origami and repeat the operation

13 - Fold one end towards the opposite side, repeat the operation on the other side

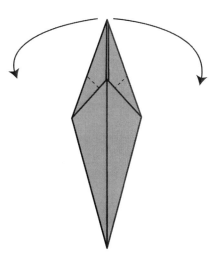

14 - Lower the tips perpendicular by reversing the fold

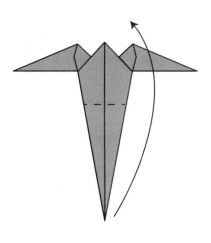

15 - Fold a tip upwards

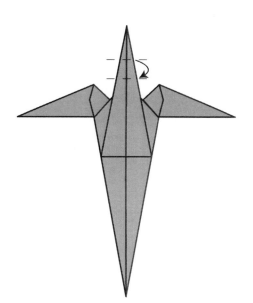

16 - Fold the tip back

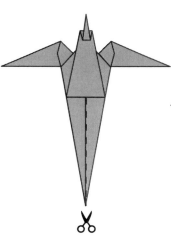

17 - Cut in the middle all the way and cross the two tips

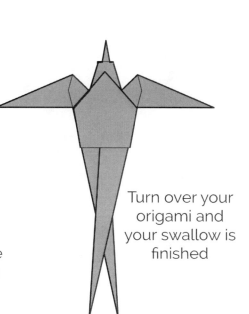

Turn over your origami and your swallow is finished

Jumping Frog

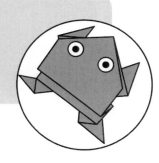

★ ★ ★

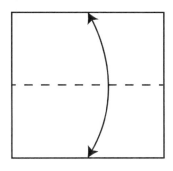

1 - Create a crease in the middle of the paper.

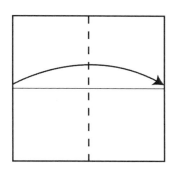

2 - Fold the paper in half in the opposite direction.

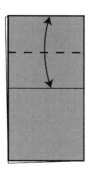

3 - Make a crease in the middle of the top half.

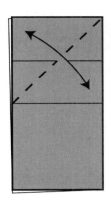

4 - Create a diagonal crease in the top half.

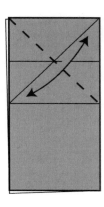

5 - Create a diagonal crease in the opposite direction.

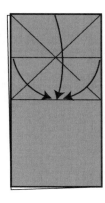

6 - Fold the top part following the previously marked creases.

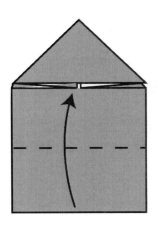

7 - Fold the bottom part in the middle.

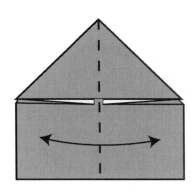

8 - Create a crease in the middle.

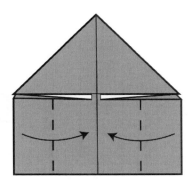

9 - Fold both sides, aligning them with the center crease.

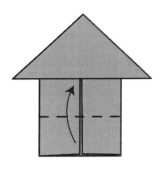

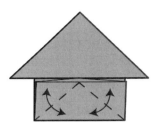

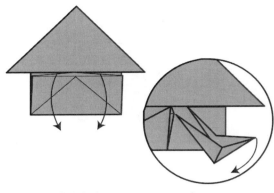

10 - Fold the bottom half upwards.

11 - Crease the folds.

12 - Unfold the corners of the bottom part, pushing them outwards.

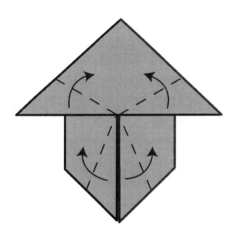

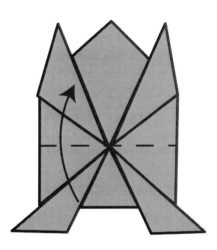

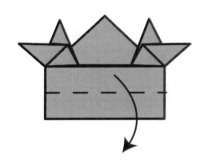

13 - Fold each extremity diagonally outward, following the dotted lines to form the legs.

14 - Fold everything in half.

15 - Fold the bottom part downward.

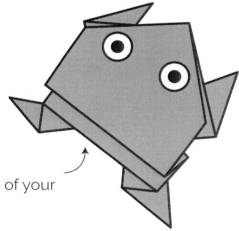

16 - Flip your origami, and you will have a jumping frog.

Press on the backside of your frog, and it will jump!

71

Parrot

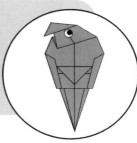

★ ★ ★

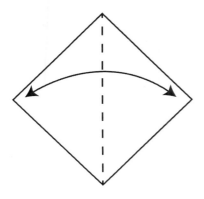

1 - Create a crease in the centre of the sheet along the diagonal.

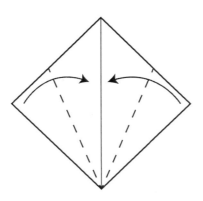

2 - Fold each corner to the central crease.

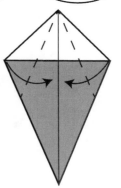

3 - Refold each corner on the central crease.

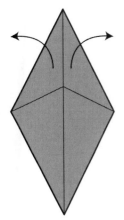

4 - Unfold your origami.

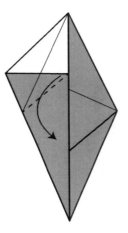

5 - Refold your origami along the dotted lines, folding downwards on each side.

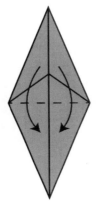

6 - Fold the top tip downwards.

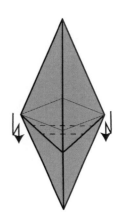

7 - Accordion fold the tips.

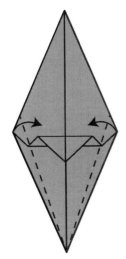

8 - Fold each corner inwards.

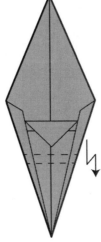

9 - Accordion fold the bottom tip.

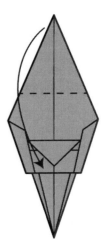

10 - Fold the top tip along the dotted lines.

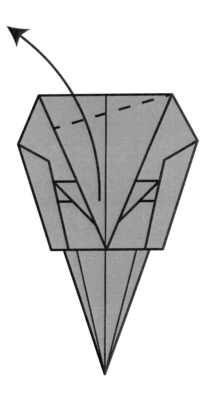

11 - Fold the top tip upwards diagonally following the dotted lines.

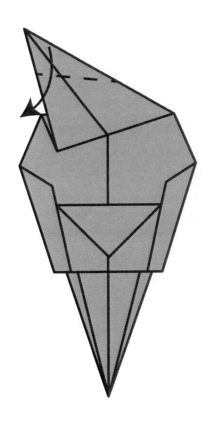

12 - Fold the tip downwards following the dotted lines to create the beak.

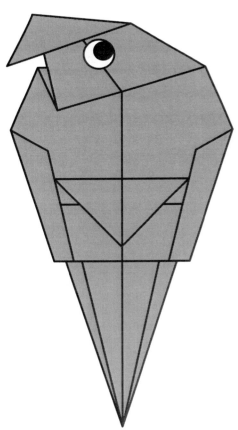

Your parrot is ready!

Reindeer

★ ★ ★

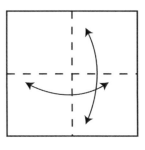

1 - Mark the folds following the dotted lines.

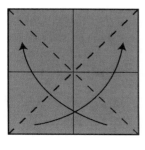

2 - Turn over your origami and mark the diagonal folds.

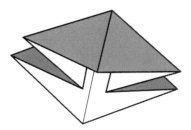

3 - Follow the fold lines and fold your origami.

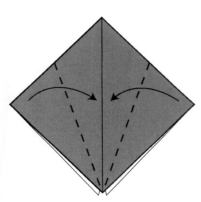

4 - With the opening facing down, fold the corners towards the center.

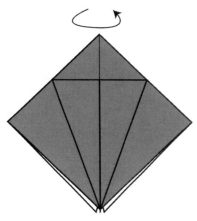

5 - Turn your origami over.

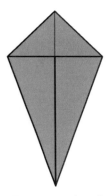

6 - Repeat the fold from step 4.

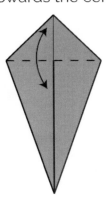

7 - Fold the top corner down following the dotted lines to mark the fold.

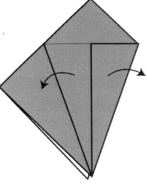

8 - Unfold the corners on both sides.

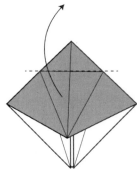
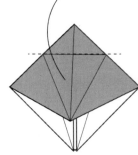

9 - Fold the bottom part upwards while flattening the corners, and repeat steps 7, 8, and 9 on the other side.

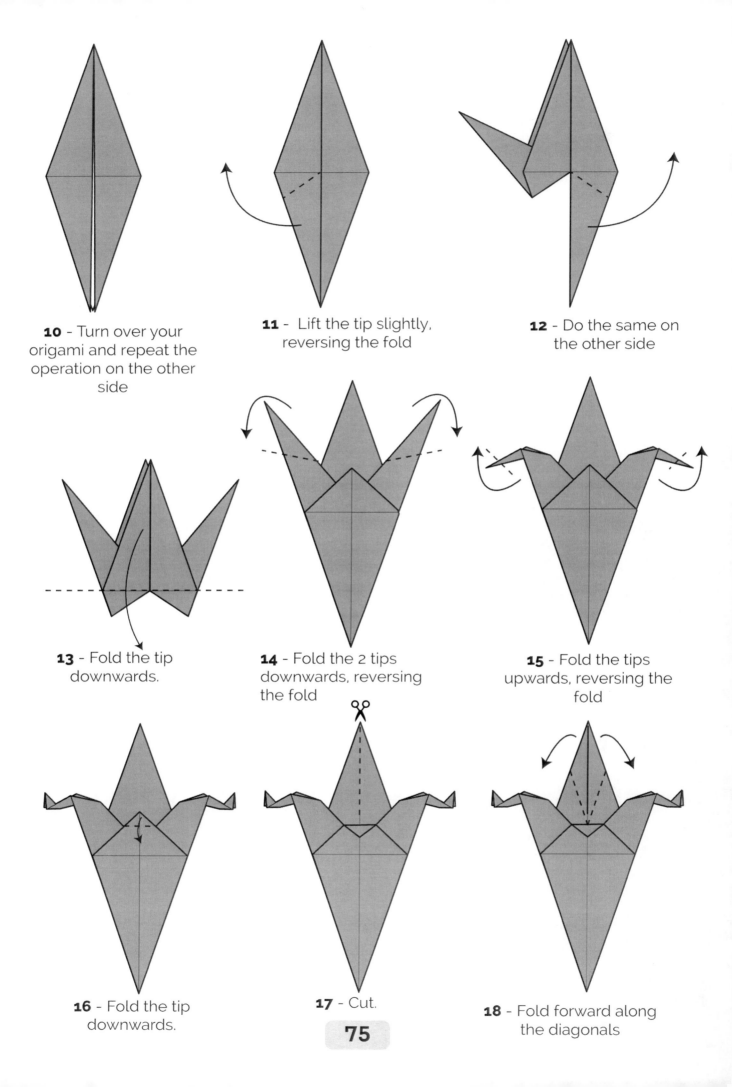

10 - Turn over your origami and repeat the operation on the other side

11 - Lift the tip slightly, reversing the fold

12 - Do the same on the other side

13 - Fold the tip downwards.

14 - Fold the 2 tips downwards, reversing the fold

15 - Fold the tips upwards, reversing the fold

16 - Fold the tip downwards.

17 - Cut.

18 - Fold forward along the diagonals

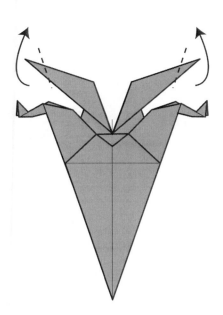

19 - Fold the tips backward on the dotted lines

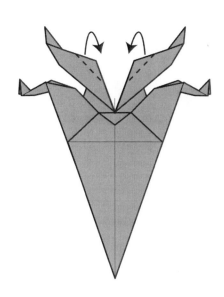

20 - Fold the tops behind

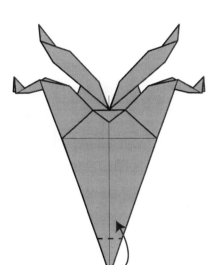

21 - Fold the tip forward

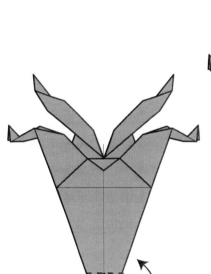

22 - Do the same

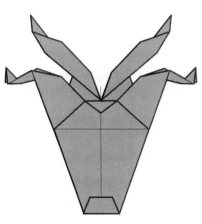

23 - Draw eyes and a nose

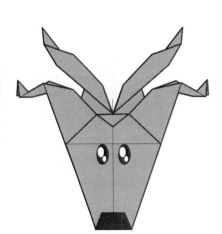

Your reindeer is finished

Rhinoceros

★ ★ ★

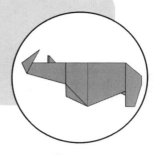

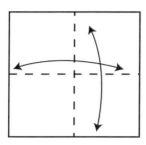

1 - Mark the fold

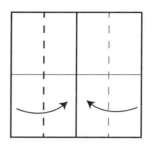

2 - Fold on the quarter

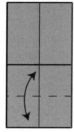

3 - Mark the folds

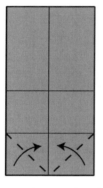

4 - Mark the fold

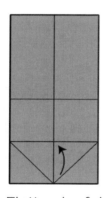

5 - Flatten by folding the corners towards the center

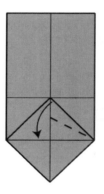

6 - Fold the tip along the center

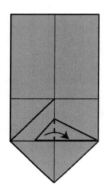

7 - Fold the part that sticks out to the side

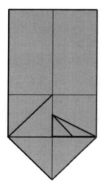

8 - Do the same on the other side

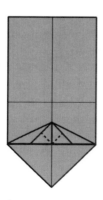

9 - Fold the small tip along the center

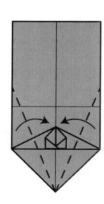

10 - Fold each end towards the center

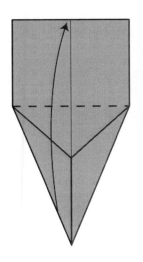

11 - Mark the fold at the tips

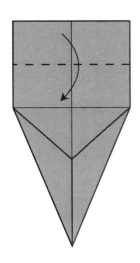

12 - Mark the fold in the middle

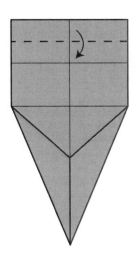

13 - Fold

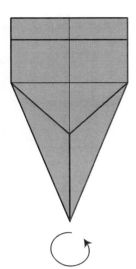

14 - Turn over

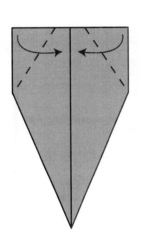

15 - Fold

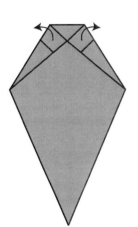

16 - Flatten the tips

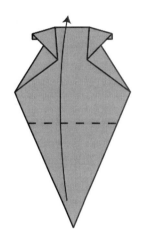

17 - Mark the fold

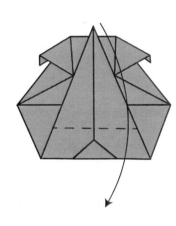

18 - Fold the tip as shown in the drawing

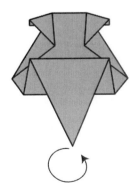

19 - Turn over your origami

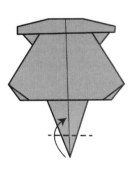

20 - Fold the end upwards

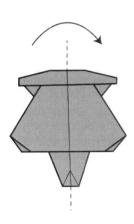

21 - Fold it in half

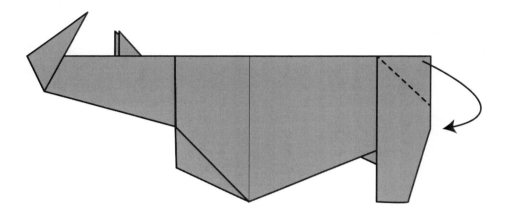

22- Bring out the small horn and tuck the back inside the fold

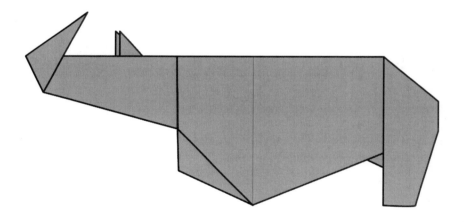

Your animal is ready.

Scorpion

★ ★ ★

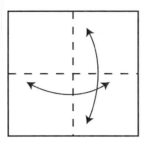

1 - Mark the folds following the dotted lines.

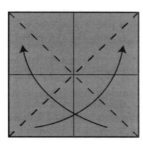

2 - Turn over your origami and mark the diagonal folds.

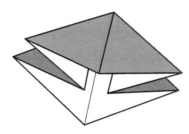

3 - Follow the construction fold direction and fold your origami.

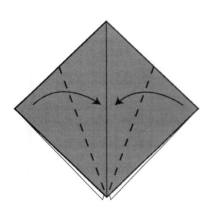

4 - With the opening facing down, fold the corners towards the center.

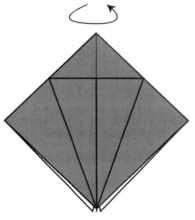

5 - Turn over your origami.

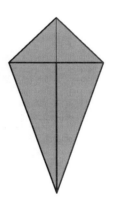

6 - Repeat the fold from step 4.

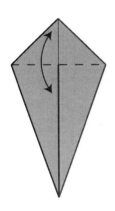

7 - Fold the top corner down following the dotted lines to mark the fold.

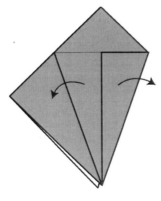

8 - Unfold the corners on both sides.

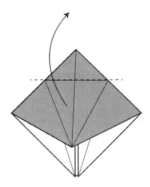

9 - RFold the bottom part upwards while squashing the corners, and repeat steps 7, 8, and 9 on the other side.

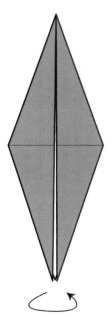

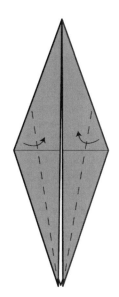

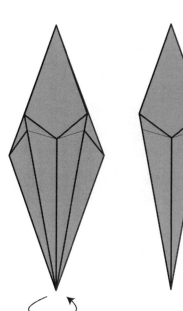

10 - Turn your origami over and repeat the operation on the other side.

11 - Keep the opening facing down and fold each corner towards the center.

12 - Turn your origami over and repeat the operation.

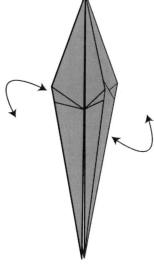

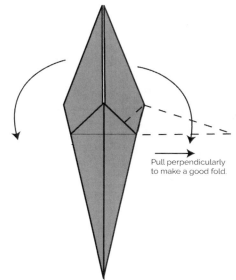

Pull perpendicularly to make a good fold.

13 - Open your origami on each side.

14 - Fold the tips horizontally, reversing the fold, on both sides.

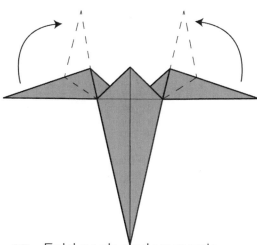

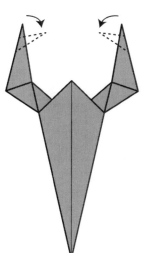

15 - Fold each end upwards, reversing the fold on both sides.

16 - Fold the tips horizontally inwards, reversing the fold on both sides.

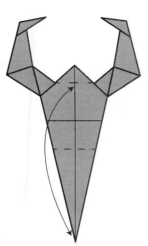

16 - Mark the fold by folding the tip upwards at the dotted lines.

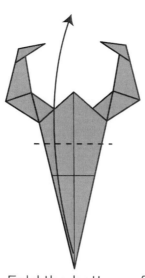

17 - Fold the bottom of the triangle towards the dotted lines.

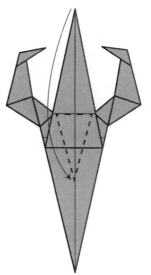

18 - Fold the tip downwards at the fold marked in step 16.

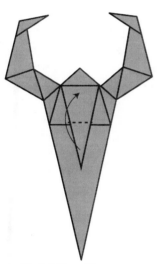

19 - Fold the tip upwards so it doesn't stick out.

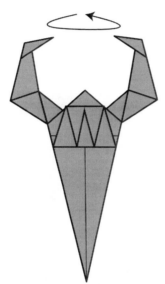

20 - Turn your origami over.

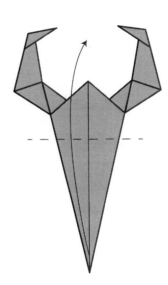

21 - Completely fold the tip upwards.

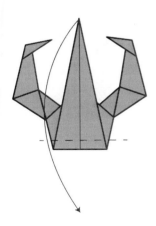

22 - Fold the tip downwards at the dotted lines.

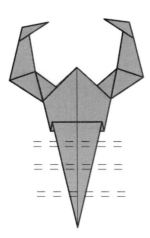

23 - Repeat the operation 3 times, moving downwards, to create an accordion shape.

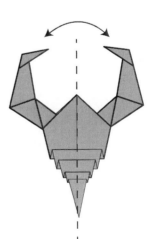

24 - Fold your origami in half.

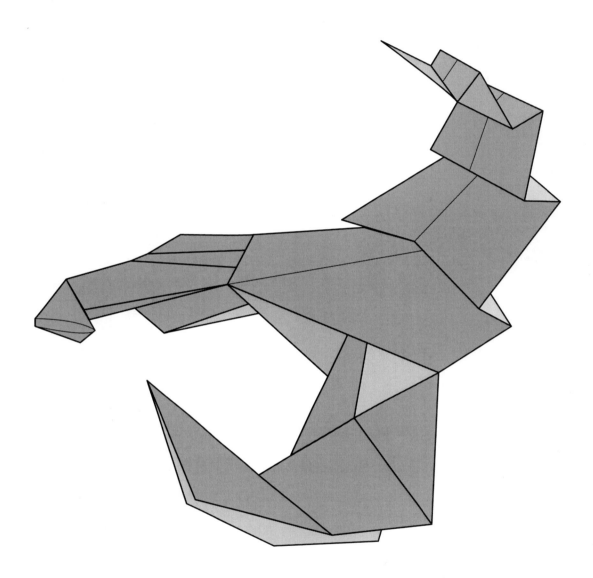

Your Scorpion is ready!

Diamond Ring

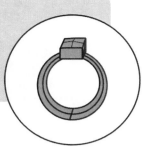

★ ☆ ☆

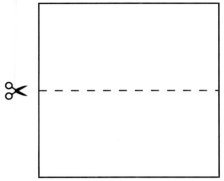

1 - Cut the sheet in half

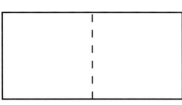

2 - Mark the vertical fold in the middle

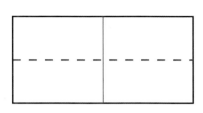

3 - Mark the horizontal fold in the middle

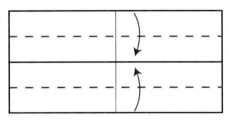

4 - Fold each end towards the centre

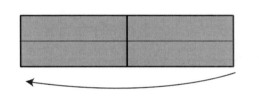

5 - Fold your origami in half

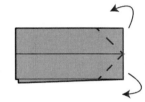

6 - Fold the corners inside, reversing the fold

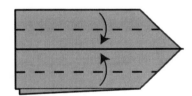

7 - Fold each end towards the centre

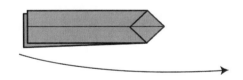

8 - Open up

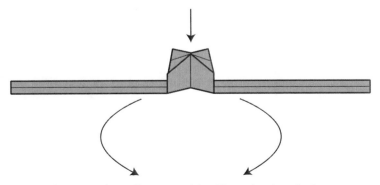

9 - Flatten the diamond to the desired shape
- Close the ring using adhesive on both ends

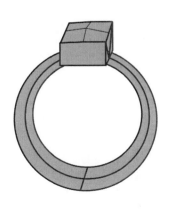

Your ring is ready!

84

Bracelet

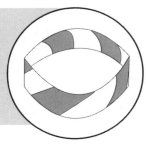

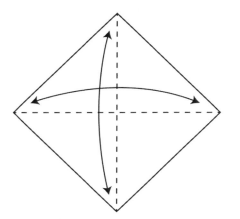

1 - Make folds in the middle of the sheet along the diagonals.

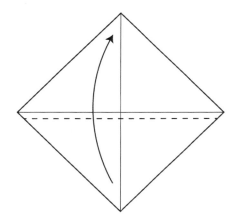

2 - Fold your sheet in half slightly below the center.

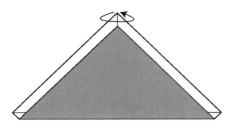

3 - Turn your origami over.

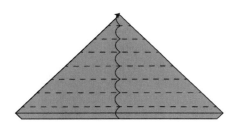

4 - Fold by wrapping your origami following the dotted lines.

5 - Wrap it around itself.

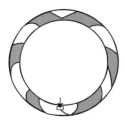

6 - Use adhesive to stick the two ends together.

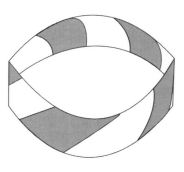

Your bracelet is ready!

Winged Heart

★ ☆ ☆

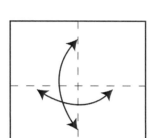

1 - Make the folds.

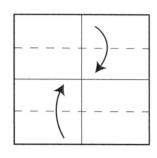

2 - Fold the two parts towards the center.

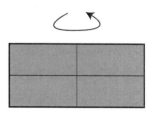

3 - Turn your origami over.

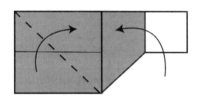
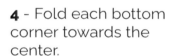

4 - Fold each bottom corner towards the center.

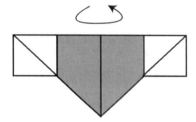

5 - Turn your origami over again.

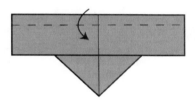

6 - Fold the top following the dotted lines.

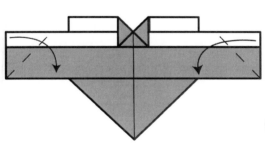

7 - Fold the two corners downwards.

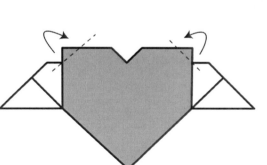

8 - Fold the two corners that will form the heart.

Your heart is ready!

86

Heart

★ ☆ ☆

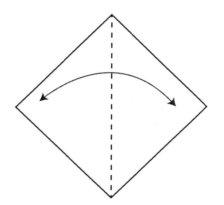

1 - Fold in the middle along the diagonal.

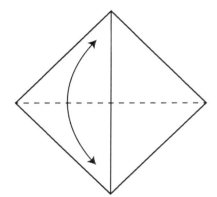

2 - Fold in the middle along the other diagonal.

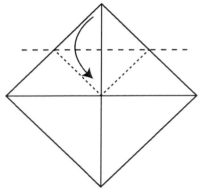

3 - Fold the top tip towards the center.

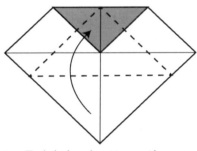

4 - Fold the bottom tip up to the top of your origami.

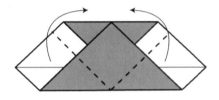

5 - Fold each end upwards to form the heart.

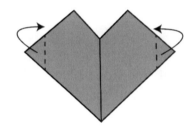

6 - Fold each end to the back.

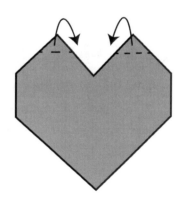

7 - Fold each end to the back again.

Your heart is ready!

Cactus

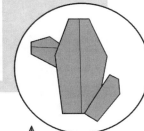

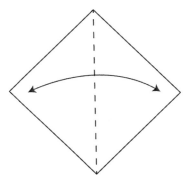

1 - Mark the fold on the diagonal

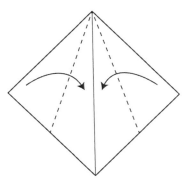

2 - Fold each end towards the centre

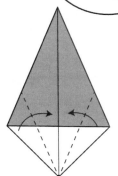

3 - Fold each end towards the centre again

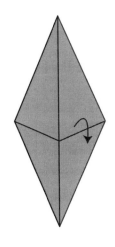

4 - Unfold the right corner

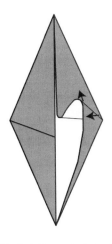

5 - Fold the right side upwards to create a tip

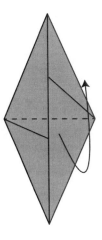

6 - Fold the bottom part to the back

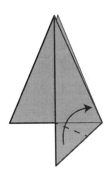

7 - Fold the tip diagonally

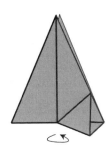

8 - Turn over your origami

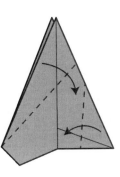

9 - Fold the tips along the dotted lines

88

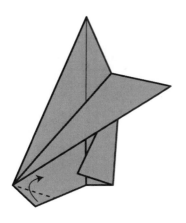

10 - Mark the fold

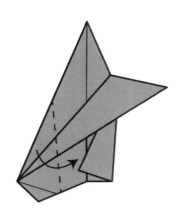

11 - Fold the left side over to the right

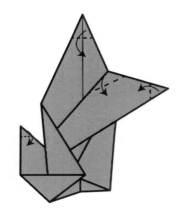

12 - Fold the tips along the dotted lines

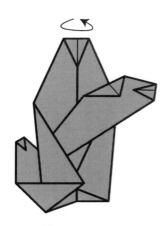

13 - Turn over your origami

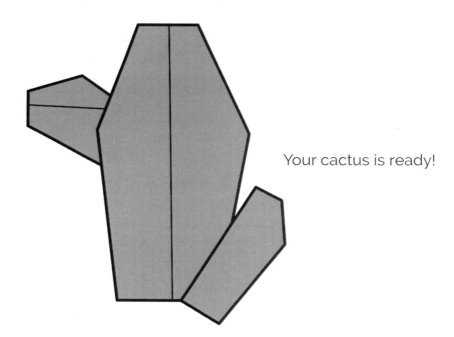

Your cactus is ready!

Windmill Flower

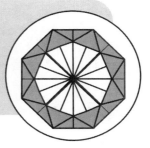

★ ★ ☆

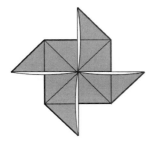

1 - Create a windmill as shown on page 108

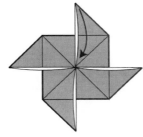

2 - Open and fold, bringing the tip towards the center

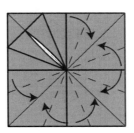

3 - Fold the corners along the diagonals

4 - Repeat for each section

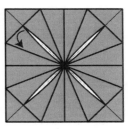

5 - Open and fold, bringing each tip towards the center of their respective diagonals

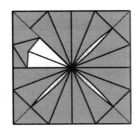

6 - Repeat for each section

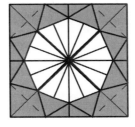

7 - Fold the corners of the square towards the back

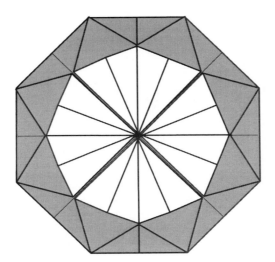

90

Your flower is complete!

Morning Glory

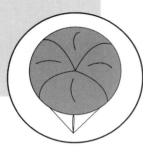

★ ★ ☆

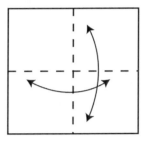

1 - Mark the folds following the dotted lines.

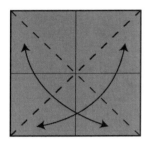

2 - Turn your origami over and mark the diagonal folds.

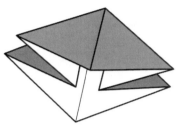

3 - Follow the fold directions and fold your origami.

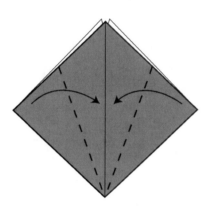

4 - Keep the opening facing up and fold the corners towards the center.

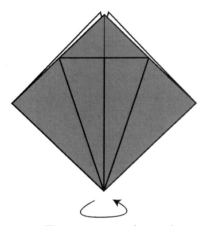

5 - Turn your origami over.

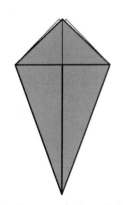

6 - Repeat the fold from step 4.

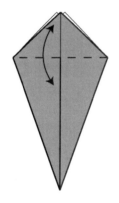

7 - Fold the top corner down following the dotted lines to mark the fold.

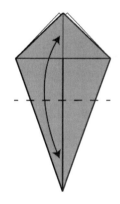

8 - Mark the fold.

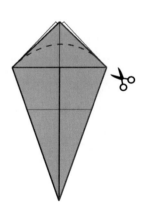

9 - Cut the top part with scissors.

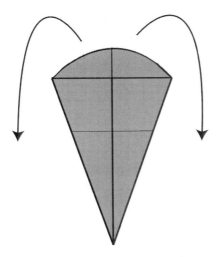

10 - Open your origami.

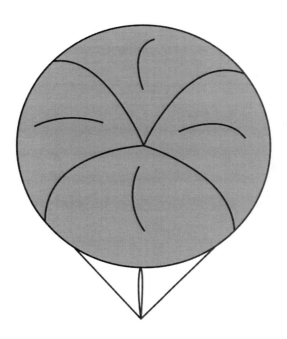

Your flower is ready!

★ ★ ☆

Iris

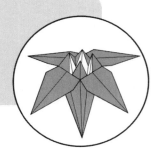

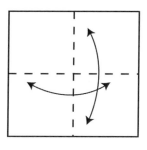

1 - Mark the folds by following the dotted lines.

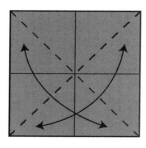

2 - Turn your origami over and mark the folds diagonally.

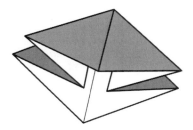

3 - Follow the direction of the construction folds and fold your origami.

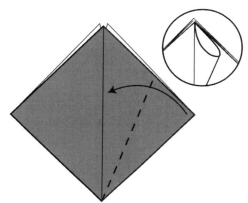

4 - Keep the opening facing down and fold the corners towards the center.

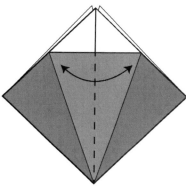

5 - Press down by opening the fold, repeat steps 4 and 5 on all petals.

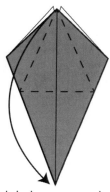

6 - Fold downwards.

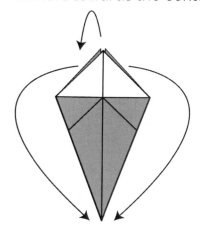

7 - Repeat the operation on all sides.

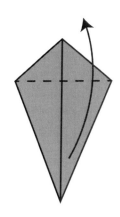

8 - Lift all the petals upwards.

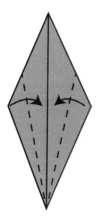

9 - Fold the ends towards the center.

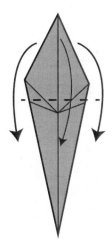

10 - Fold down all the petals.

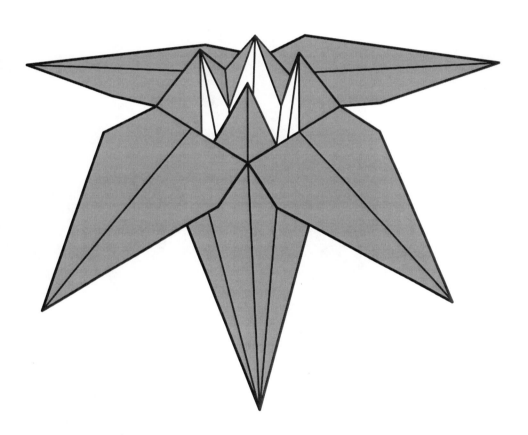

Your flower is ready!

Water Lily

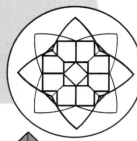

★ ★ ☆

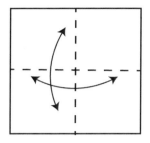

1 - Mark the creases

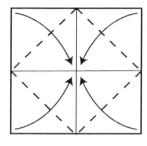

2 - Fold the corners towards the center

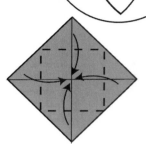

3 - Fold the corners towards the center

4 - Fold the corners towards the center

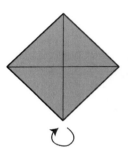

5 - Turn over

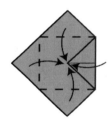

6 - Fold the corners towards the center

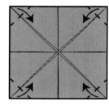

7 - Partially fold the corners towards the center

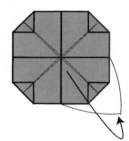

8 - Curl the 1st layer by pushing in the corner and pulling the petal outwards

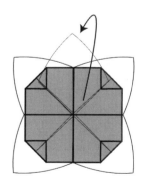

9 - Repeat for the 2nd layer

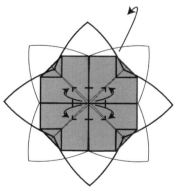

10 - Fold the center tips outwards. Your water lily is complete!

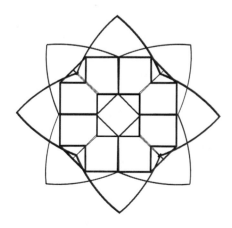

Rose

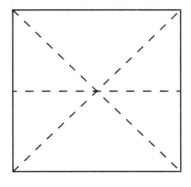

1 - Mark the creases

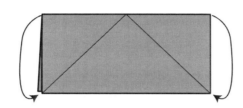

2 - Reverse the corner folds

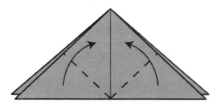

3 - Fold the top along the crease

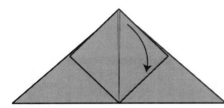

4 - Collapse the top along the line

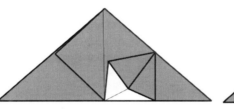

5 - Fold the central bottom corners on their diagonal

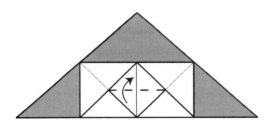

6 - Fold down the bottom part of the central triangle

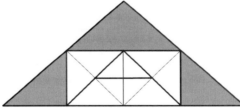

7 - Repeat steps 4, 5, and 6 on the opposite side

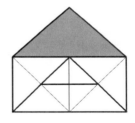

8 - Close the two faces and open the sides

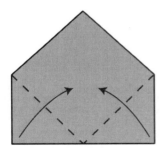

9 - Fold the corners along their diagonal

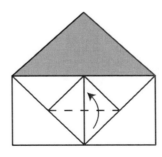

10 - Fold down the bottom part of the central triangle

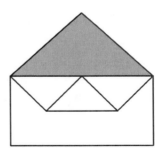

11- Repeat steps 9 and 10 on the opposite side

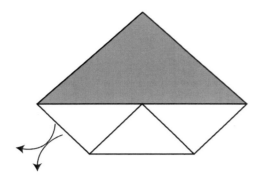

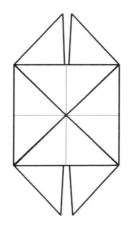

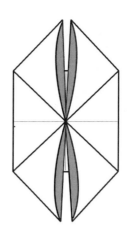

12 - Open the bottom parte

13 - View from below

14 - View from the top

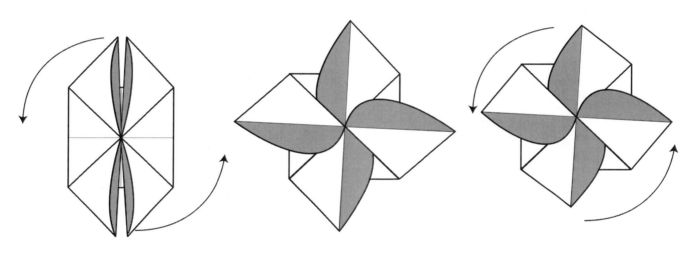

15 - Twist as if you're screwing in the tip

16 - Lift the tips

17 - Continue twisting

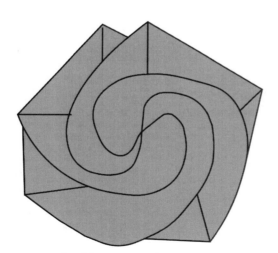

18 - Your rose is complete

*For a better finish, consider using single-coloured paper.

Pumpkin

★ ☆ ☆

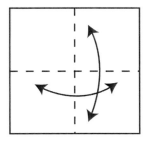

1 - Mark the folds following the dotted lines.

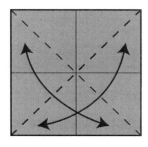

2 - Turn your origami over and mark the folds diagonally.

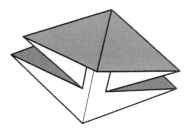

3 - Follow the direction of the construction folds and fold your origami.

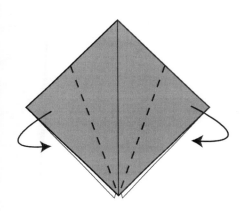

4 - Keep the opening facing down and fold the corners inwards following the dotted lines.

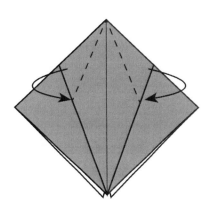

5 - Fold the top in the same way inwards.

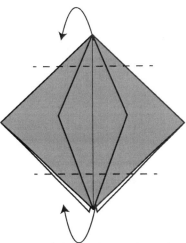

6 - Fold each end to the back following the dotted lines.

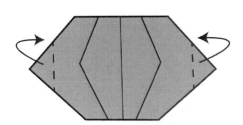

7 - Fold each side end to the back following the dotted lines.

Draw a face on it, and your pumpkin is ready!

Ghost

★ ☆ ☆

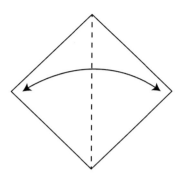

1 - Mark the fold on the diagonal.

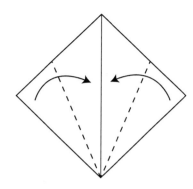

2 - Fold each end towards the center.

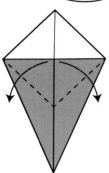

3 - Fold the corners outwards.

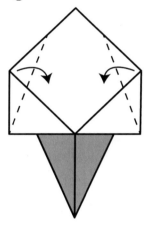

4 - Fold both ends inward.

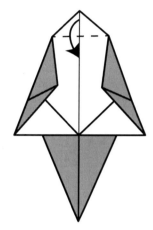

5 - Fold the top corner downwards.

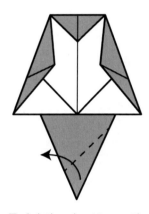

6 - Fold the bottom tip diagonally following the dotted lines.

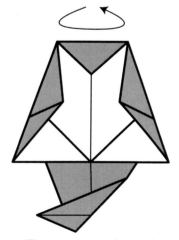

7 - Turn your origami over.

Draw eyes and a mouth, and your ghost will be ready!

Frankenstein

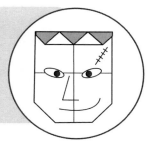

★ ☆ ☆

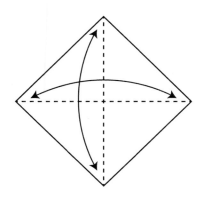

1 - Mark the folds on the diagonals.

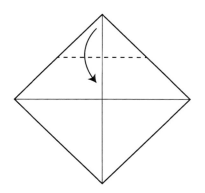

2 - Fold the tip downwards following the dotted lines.

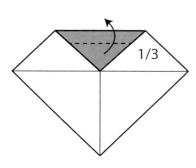

1/3

3 - Lift the tip following the dotted lines.

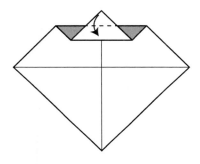

4 - Fold the tip back down.

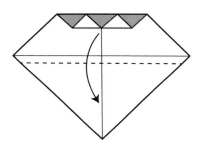

5 - Fold down the top part.

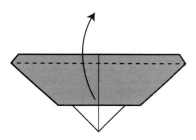

6 - Lift following the dotted lines.

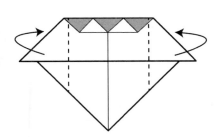

7 - Fold the ends to the back.

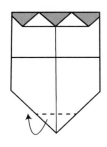

8 - Fold the bottom tip to the back.

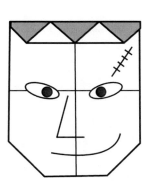

Frankenstein's creature is ready!

Witch

★ ☆ ☆

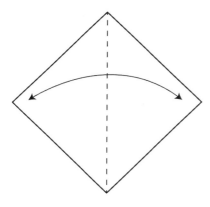

1 - Mark the fold in the center on the diagonal.

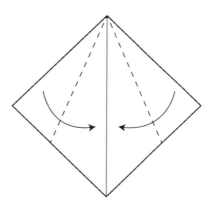

2 - Fold the ends towards the center.

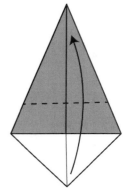

3 - Fold the bottom part upwards.

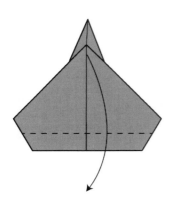

4 - Fold downwards following the dotted lines.

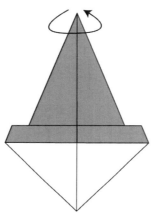

5 - Turn over your origami.

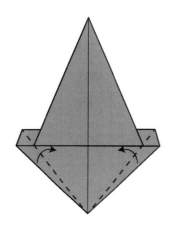

6 - Fold the ends inwards following the dotted lines.

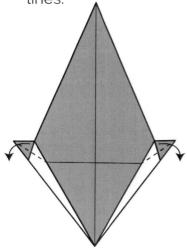

7 - Fold the corners outward by opening the folds.

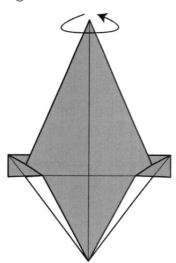

8 - Turn over your origami.

Draw a face on it, and your witch is ready!

Skull

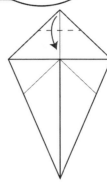

★ ★ ☆

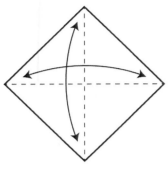

1 - Mark the folds in the center on the diagonals.

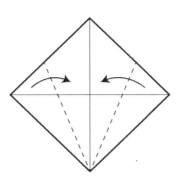

2 - Fold the ends towards the center.

3 - Fold the tip downwards following the dotted lines.

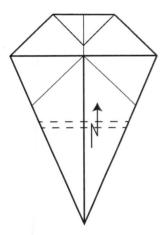

4 - Fold the bottom part like an accordion.

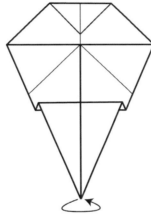

5 - Turn over your origami.

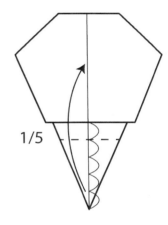

1/5

6 - Fold the bottom part upwards.

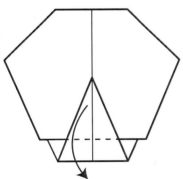

7 - Fold the tip following the dotted lines.

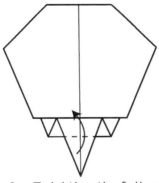

8 - Fold the tip following the dotted lines.

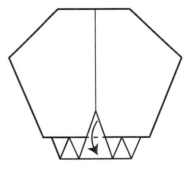

9 - Fold the tip following the dotted lines.

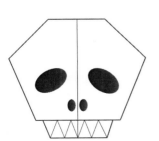

Your skull is ready!

102

Dracula

★ ★ ☆

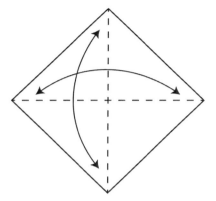

1 - Mark the folds on the diagonals.

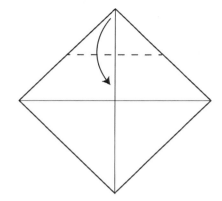

2 - Fold the tip towards the center.

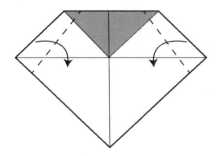

3 - Fold the ends inwards.

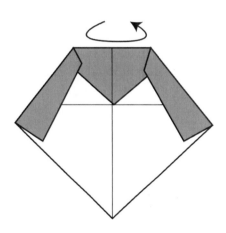

4 - Turn over your origami.

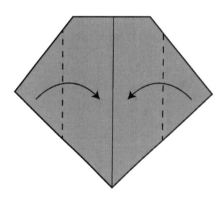

5 - Fold the ends towards the center.

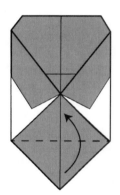

6 - Fold the tip upwards.

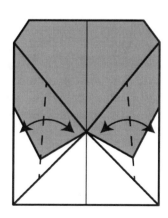

7 - Mark the folds.

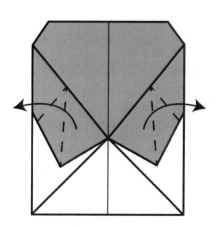

8 - Fold outwards while opening the fold.

103

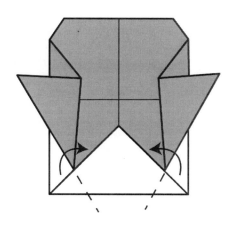

9 - Fold the corners inwards to create the jaw.

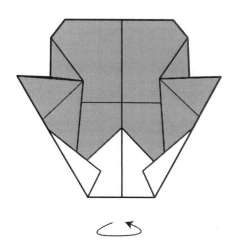

10 - Turn your origami over.

Draw a face on it and Dracula is ready!

Paper Fortune Teller

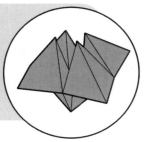

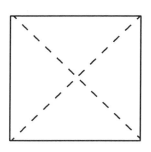

1 - Mark the folds

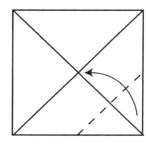

2 - Fold the corners to the center

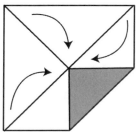

3 - Repeat for each corner

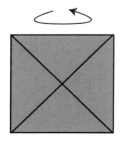

4 - Turn it over

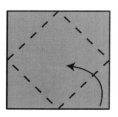

5 - Fold the corners to the centre again

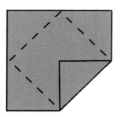

6 - Repeat for each corner

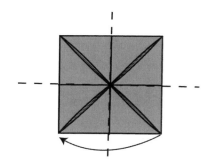

7 - Join the 4 corners together and open the 4 bottom sections

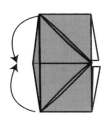

8 - Mark the folds again and fold it in half

9 - Your paper fortune teller is finished. All that's left is to decide on the challenges and questions to ask

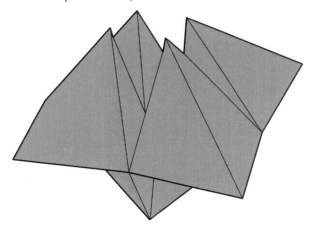

105

Crown

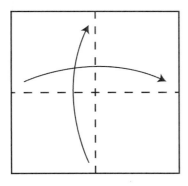

1 - Mark the folds

2 - Fold the ends towards the centre diagonally

3 - Fold the bottom part in half

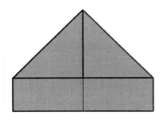
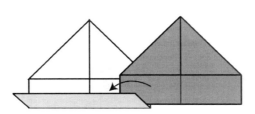
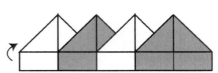

4 - Repeat several times to make a large crown

5 - Slot the pieces together

6 - Fold the bottom part and then turn it over

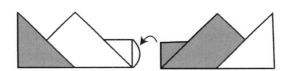

7 - Close by joining the two ends together

8 - Thread one end into the gap of the other end

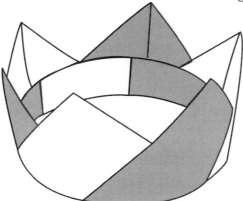

9 - You have assembled your crown

Menko Ddakji

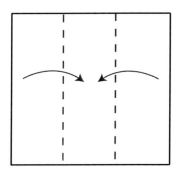

1 - Fold into thirds

2 - Fold the corners

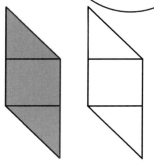

3 - Make 2 pieces

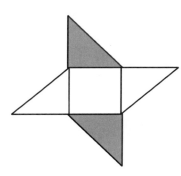

4 - Overlay the 2 pieces (identical side up)

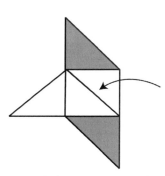

5 - Fold one triangle

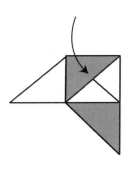

6 - Fold the 2nd triangle counter-clockwise

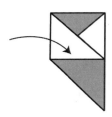

7 - Repeat with the 3rd triangle

8 - Tuck the last triangle under the first to close the origami.

9 - Slot the points into their respective notches

About Menko and Ddakji:

Menko or Ddakji are similar games. The goal of the game is to flip as many of the opponent's cards as possible using one's own card. Cards are laid on a flat surface. Each player takes turns tossing their card to flip the opponent's card using a specific technique. The player who flips the most cards wins. Menko is Japanese, while Ddakji is Korean. Menko can be played with several cards laid on the ground. Each player wins in turn the number of cards flipped.

Windmill

★ ☆ ☆

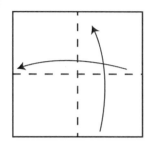

1 - Make a fold.

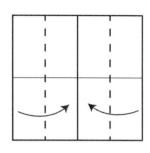

2 - Fold into a quarter

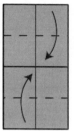

3 - Mark the folds

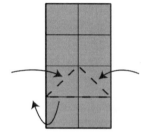

4 - Lift the bottom vertically and fold at the angles, then flatten

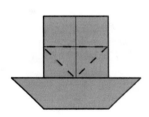

5 - Repeat the same step on the other side

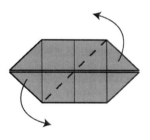

6 - Fold the tips towards the angles

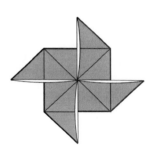

7 - Your windmill is ready

Pin it to a stick and place it in the wind.
Make sure to open the slits properly

Easy Shuriken

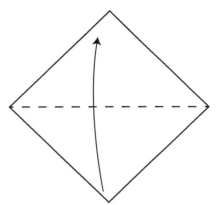

1 - Make a fold

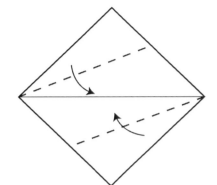

2 - Fold along the diagonals

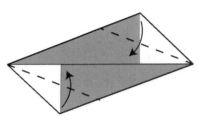

3 - Fold each part towards the centre

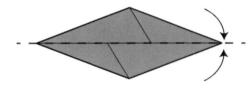

4 - Fold in half

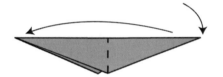

5 - Fold in half, in the opposite direction

6 - Repeat the step 4 times

Version 1:

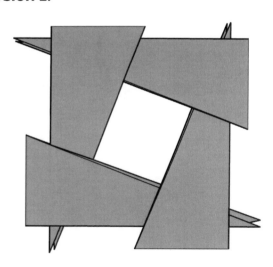

7 - Insert each tip into the slit of the opposite triangle - Ensure a central square is formed using the 4 triangles

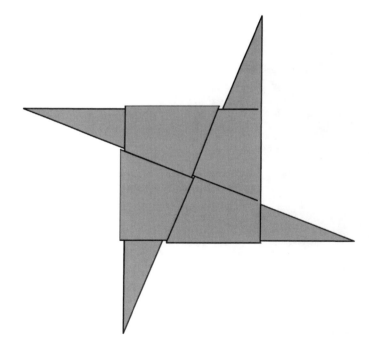

109

Version 2:

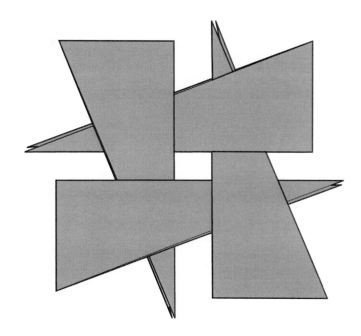

7 bis - Insert each tip into the slit of the opposite triangle
- Ensure the triangles have their right angles
positioned on each half of the figure

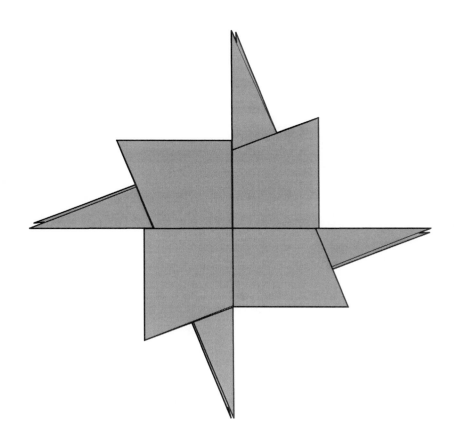

Your shurikens are complete

Shuriken

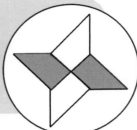

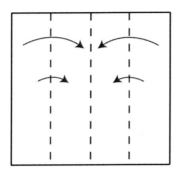

1 - Mark the fold

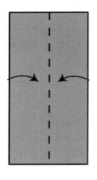

2 - Fold in half

3 - Mark the fold

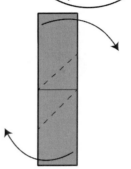

4 - Fold the ends horizontally

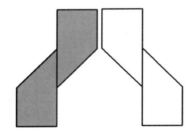

5 - Repeat the process with a sheet of another colour

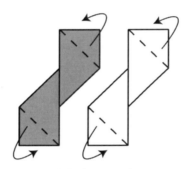

6 - Fold the point

7 - Overlay the two sheets back to back

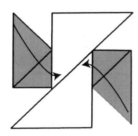

8 - Slot the points into their respective notches

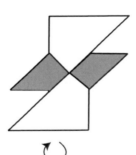

9 - Turn over

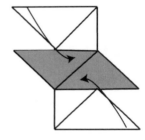

10 - Slot the points into their respective notches

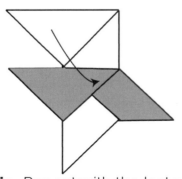

10 bis- Repeat with the last point

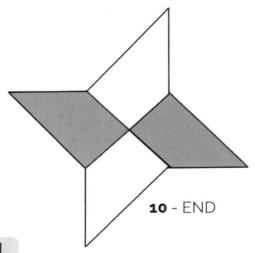

10 - END

Santa Hat

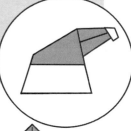

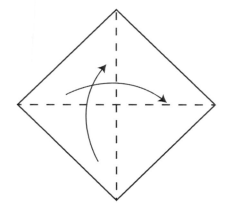

1 - Create fold lines

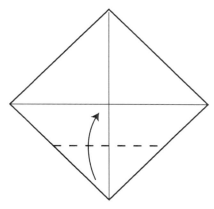

2 - Fold the tip towards the center

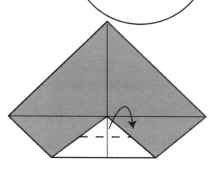

3 - Fold in half towards the inside

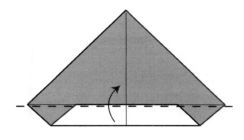

4 - Fold the bottom part upwards

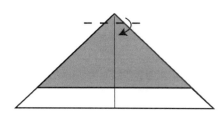

5 - Fold the top downwards

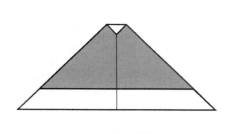

6 - Turn over

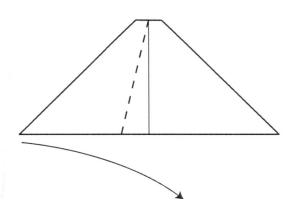

7 - Fold near the center on the diagonal

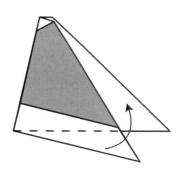

8 - Fold any excess part upwards

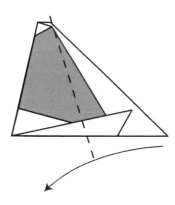

9 - Repeat on the other side

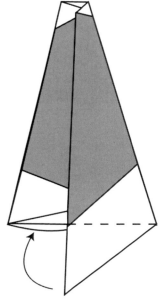

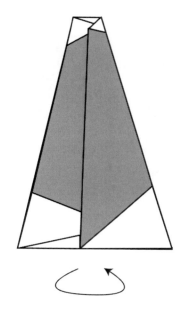

10 - Fold the part that's sticking out into the shape

11 - Turn over

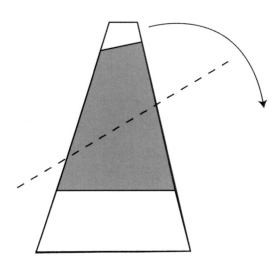

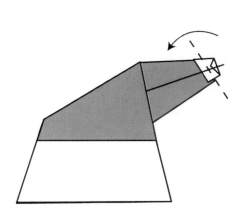

12 - Fold along the diagonal to the back

13 - Fold along the diagonal to the front

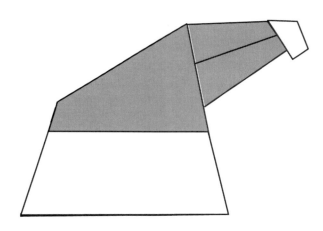

Your Santa Hat is complete

Rosette

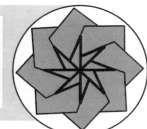

★ ☆ ☆

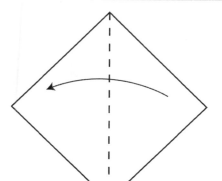

1 - Fold along
one diagonal

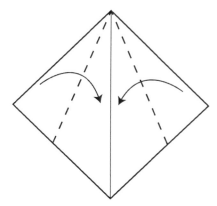

2 - Fold the ends towards
the center

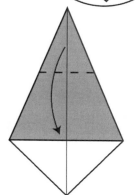

3 - Create the
fold lines

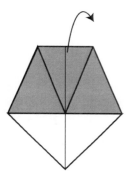

4 - Fold backwards

5 - Make 8 folds of
this type

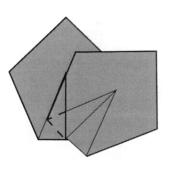

6 - Slot the petals
into a single corner

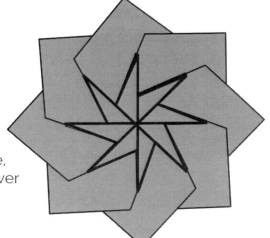

7 - To close the structure,
the first petal should be over
the last one

Your rosette is finished

114

Elf

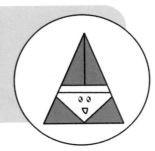

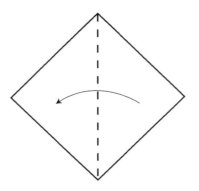

1 - Mark the fold

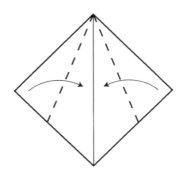

2 - Fold the ends towards the centre

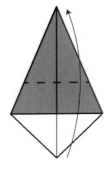

3 - Fold the bottom part upwards

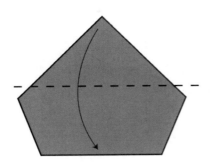

4 - Fold the top part downwards

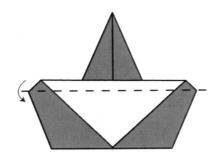

5 - Fold downwards

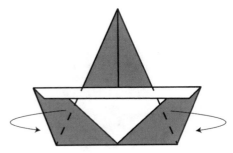

6 - Fold the ends towards the back

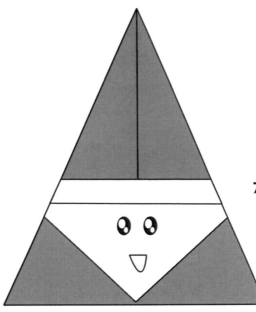

7 - Draw a face and your elf o rigami is ready

Christmas Bear

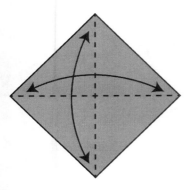

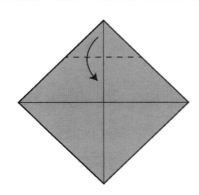

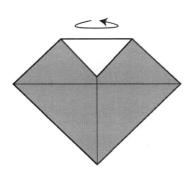

1 - Mark the folds in the center of the sheet on the diagonals.

2 - Fold the tip downwards, following the dotted lines.

3 - Turn over your origami.

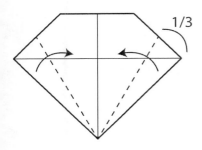

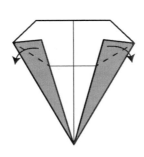

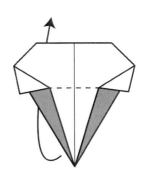

4 - Fold the ends, following the dotted lines.

5 - Fold the corners, following the dotted lines.

6 - Fold the bottom part upwards to the back at the dotted lines.

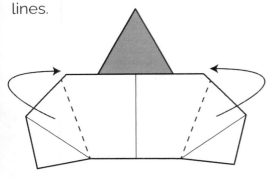

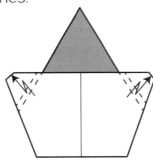

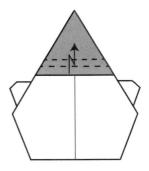

7 - Fold both ends to the back, following the dotted lines.

8 - Accordion fold the corners to create the ears.

9 - Accordion fold the top corner to create the hat.

Your Christmas bear is ready!

Santa Claus

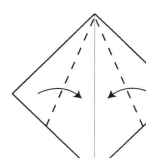

1 - Fold along the crease

2 - Fold the corners towards the center

3 - Create the fold lines

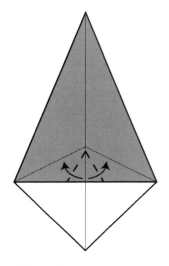

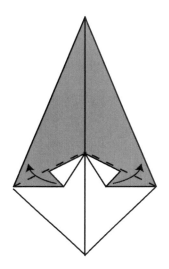

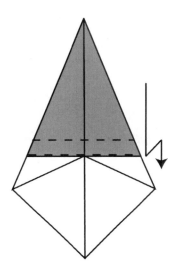

4 - Fold the corners along the marking

5 - Fold the remaining part along the crease

6 - Accordion fold the top part

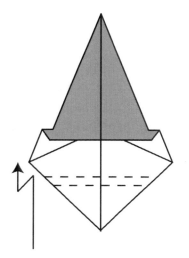

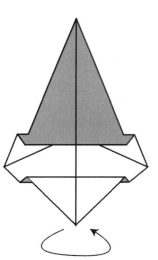

7 - Fold over with an accordion style

8 - Turn over

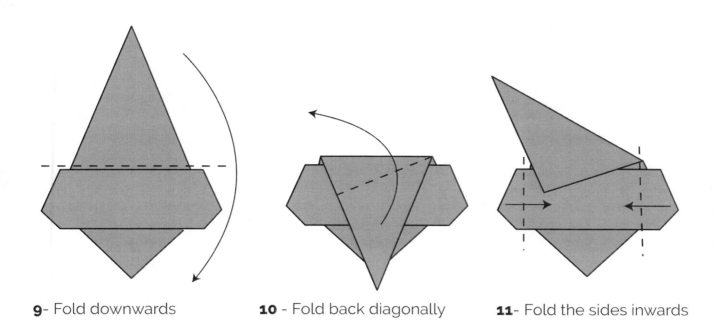

9- Fold downwards

10 - Fold back diagonally

11- Fold the sides inwards

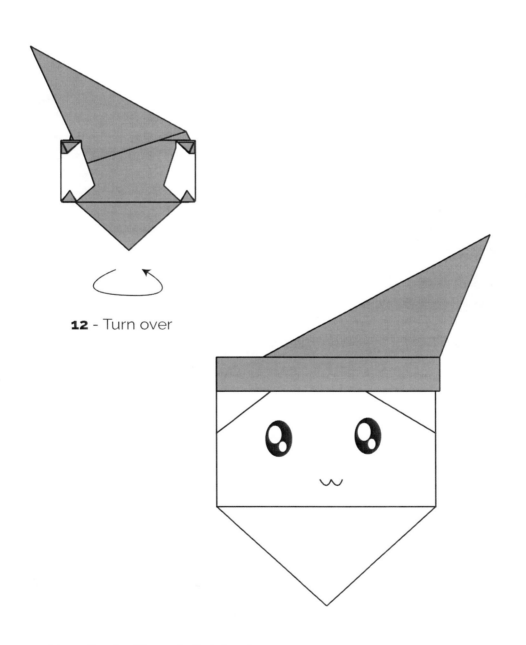

12 - Turn over

13 - Your Santa Claus is finished

Candy Cane

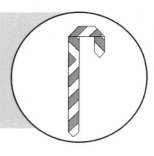

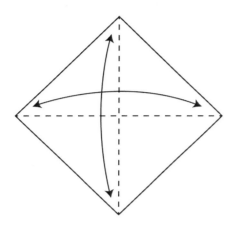

1 - Mark the folds in the middle of the sheet on the diagonals.

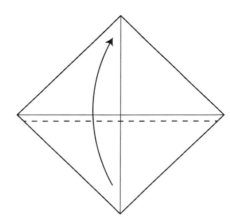

2 - Fold your sheet in half, slightly below the center.

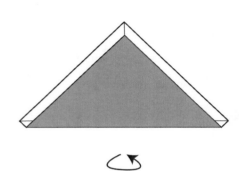

3 - Turn over your origami.

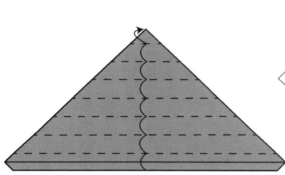

4 - Fold by rolling your origami, following the dotted lines.

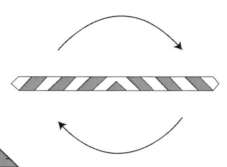

5 - Straighten your origami.

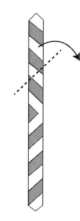

6 - Fold the end following the dotted lines.

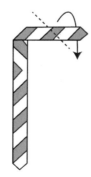

7 - Fold the end backwards, following the dotted lines.

Your candy cane is ready!

Christmas Tree

★ ☆ ☆

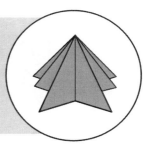

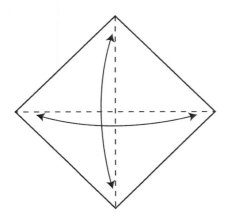

1 - Mark the folds in the center of the sheet on the diagonals.

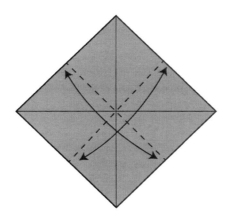

2 - Mark the folds in the center of the sheet diagonally on the other side.

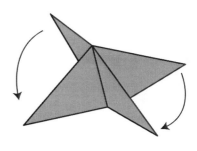

3 - Fold everything according to the construction fold direction to make a triangle.

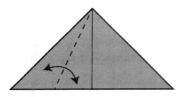

4 - Mark the fold by folding the ends towards the center.

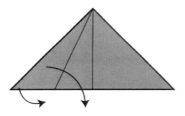

5 - Fold inward slightly opening the fold.

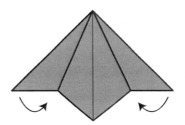

6 - Repeat on all ends.

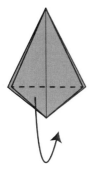

7 - Fold the lower parts inward.

8 - Open your origami in a circle.

Your tree is ready to be decorated!

120

Snowman

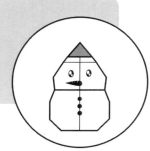

★ ★ ☆

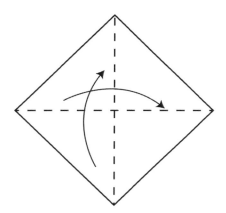

1 - Mark the folds

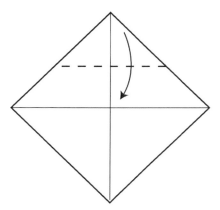

2 - Fold the tip towards the center

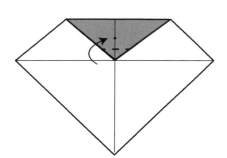

3 - Fold the tip halfway down

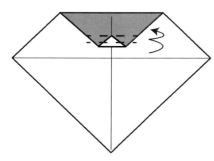

4 -Fold by wrapping around

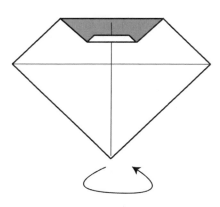

5 - Turn over

1/3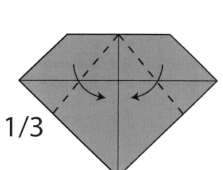

6 - Fold diagonally at about 1/3

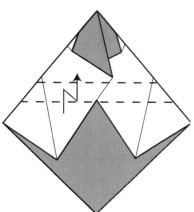

7 - Fold the bottom in an accordion style over the top part

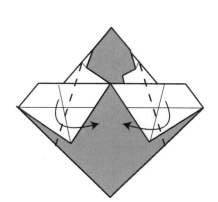

8 - Fold inwards

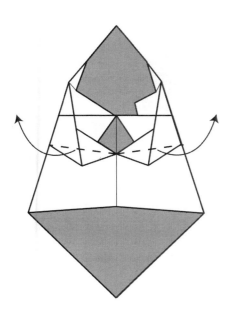

9 - Fold, opening towards
the outside

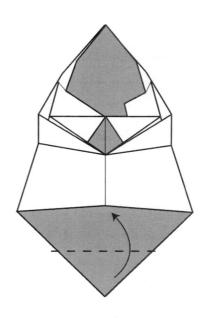

10 - Fold the tip downwards,
aligning with the center

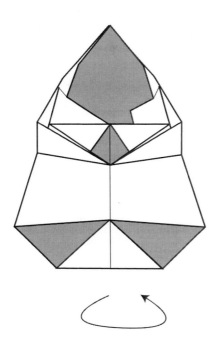

11 - Turn over

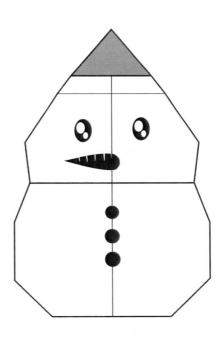

12 - Draw a face and your
origami is complete

Christmas Boot

★ ★ ☆

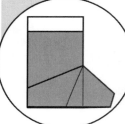

1 - Create a fold

2 - Fold in half

3 - Fold the corners towards the centre

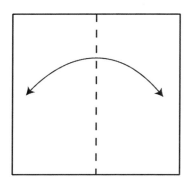

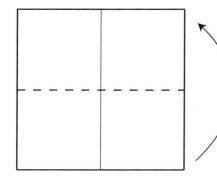

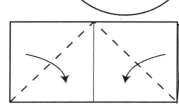

4 - Mark the fold by bending the corner perpendicular to the base

5 - Repeat on the other side

6 - Fold the top from the markings towards the centre, forming a tip

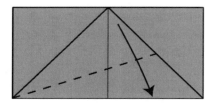

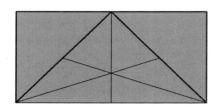

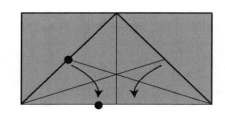

7 - Fold the protruding tip to the left side

8 - Fold to create a band at the top

9 - Turn over

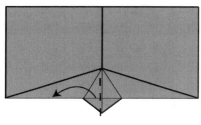

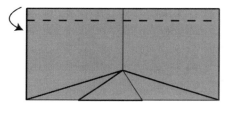

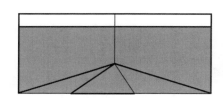

10 - Create a fold in the middle

11- Fold the sides to their halfway point

12 - Fold the sides again to close the origami

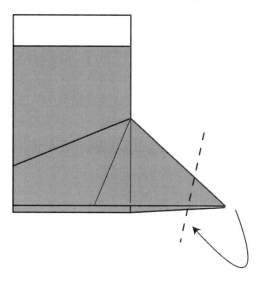

13 - Fold the end of the boot inwards

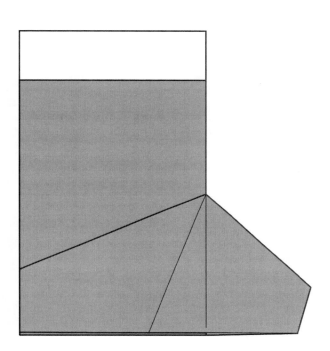

14 - Your boot is complete

★ ☆ ☆

Glider

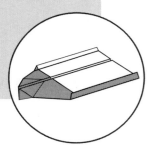

Use an A4 sheet of paper.

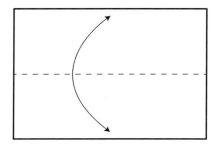

1 - Mark the fold in the center of the paper.

2 - Fold one corner along the diagonal.

3 - Fold the other corner in the same way.

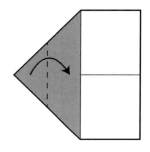

4 - Fold the tip towards the marking fold at the center of the sheet.

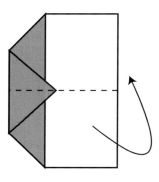

5 - Fold your origami in half lengthwise.

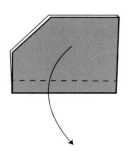

6 - Fold the wings down.

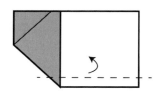

7 - Fold the bottom of the wings on both sides following the dotted lines.

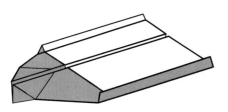

Your airplane is ready to take off!

125

Airplane

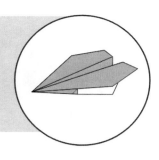

Use an A4 sheet of paper.

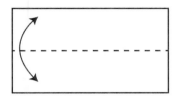

1 - Mark the fold in the center of the paper.

2 - Fold the corners towards the center on the construction fold made previously.

3 - Fold the tip towards the center following the dotted lines.

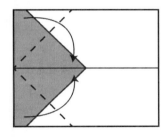

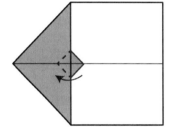

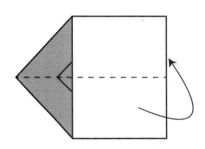

4 - Fold the tips towards the center again.

5 - Fold the tip inside.

6 - Fold your origami in half.

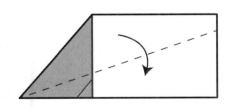

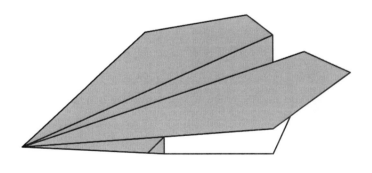

7 - Fold the wings following the dotted lines.

Your airplane is ready to fly!

Urban
Simple Airplane

★ ☆ ☆

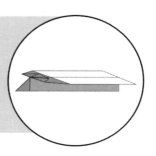

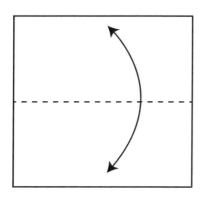

1 - Mark the fold in the center of the paper.

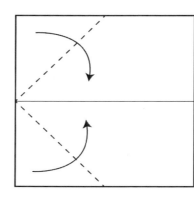

2 - Fold each corner towards the center.

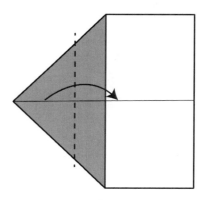

3 - Fold the tip towards the construction fold in the center following the dotted lines.

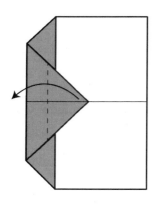

4 - Fold the tip back in the opposite direction.

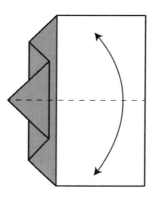

5 - Fold your origami in half.

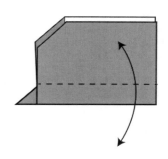

6 - Lower the wings.

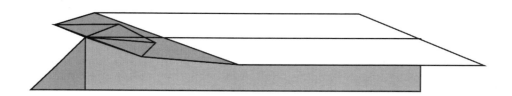

Your plane is ready to fly!

Private Jet

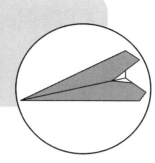

★ ☆ ☆

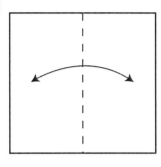

1 - Mark the fold in the center.

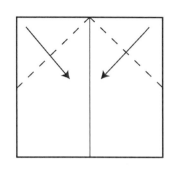

2 - Fold the corners towards the center.

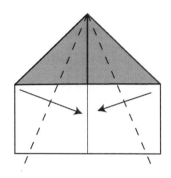

3 - Fold each end back to the center.

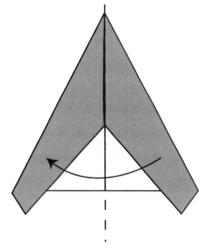

4 - Fold your origami in half.

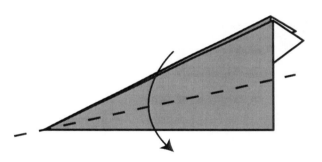

5 - Fold each wing downwards.

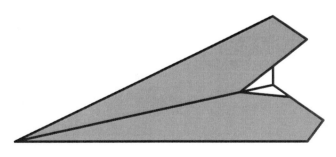

Your plane is ready to fly!

128

Fishing Boat

★ ☆ ☆

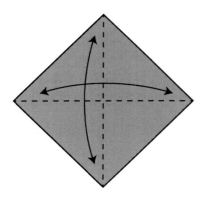

1 - Mark the folds on the diagonals.

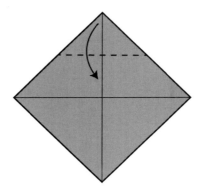

2 - Fold the tip towards the center of the sheet.

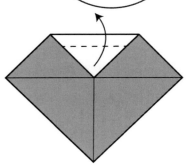

3 - Lift the tip following the dotted lines.

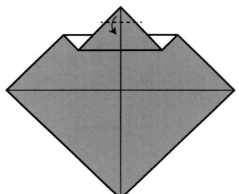

4 - Lower the tip downwards following the dotted lines.

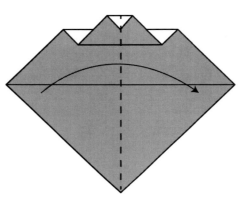

5 - Fold your origami in half.

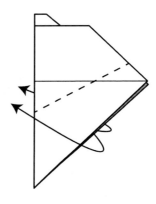

6 - Lift the bottom by reversing the fold.

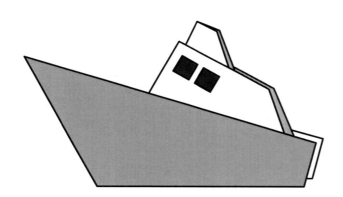

Your fishing boat is ready!

Boat

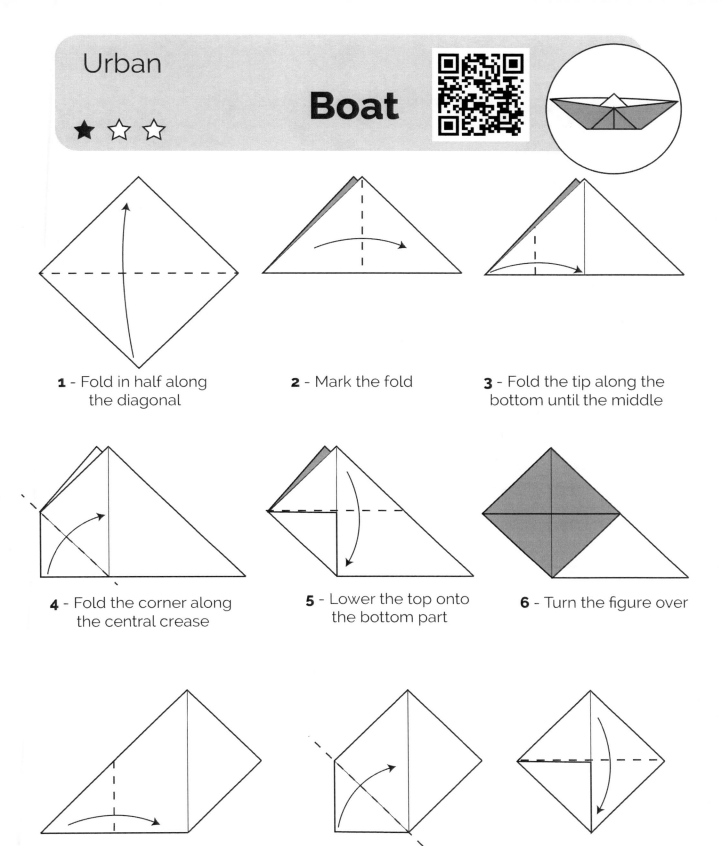

1 - Fold in half along the diagonal

2 - Mark the fold

3 - Fold the tip along the bottom until the middle

4 - Fold the corner along the central crease

5 - Lower the top onto the bottom part

6 - Turn the figure over

7 - Repeat steps 3, 4, and 5 on the other side

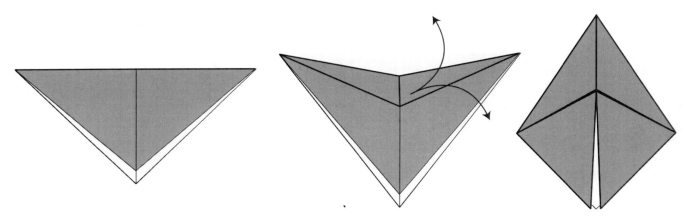

8 - Turn the figure over again

9 - Reverse the folds by opening the folding and pivot by 90°

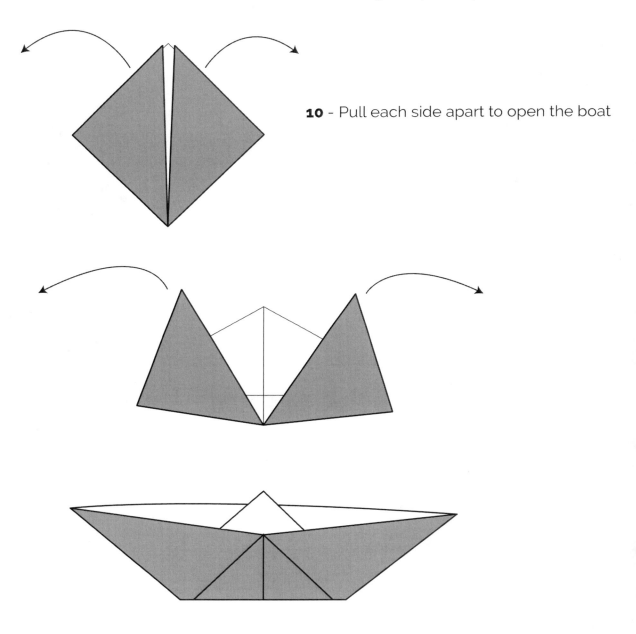

10 - Pull each side apart to open the boat

Your boat is complete

Small boat

★ ☆ ☆

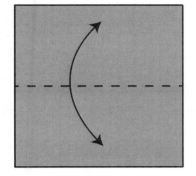

1 - Mark the fold

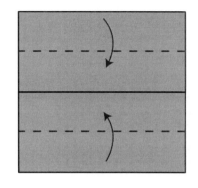

2 - Fold both halves in two.

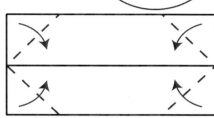

3 - Fold each corner

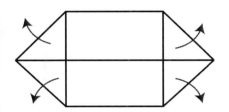

4 - Unfold

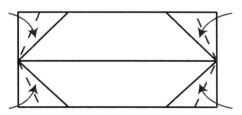

5 - Mark the folds

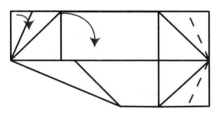

6 - Tuck the small corner inside so it's hidden
- Fold the larger corner over half of the fold

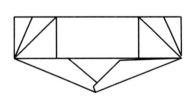

7 - Repeat on the opposite side
- Overlap the two folds
- Repeat for the remaining corners

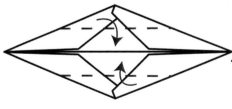

8 - Fold the two tops towards the centre

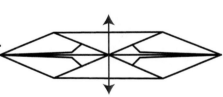

9 - Open up

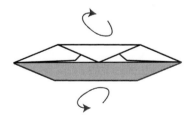

10- Roll up the entire piece like a sock

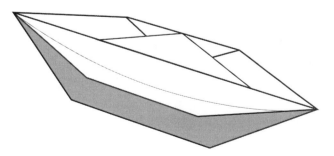

11- Invert the peaks inwardly.

Your boat is ready to set sail.

Little Boat

★ ☆ ☆

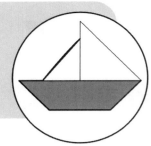

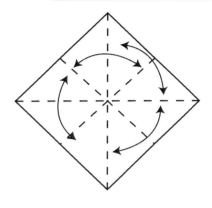

1 - Mark the folds and then fold the sides inwards

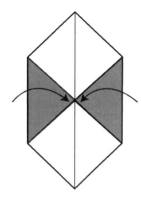

2 - Close the figure in half

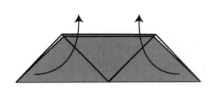

3 - Fold the peaks inwards

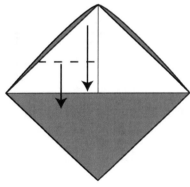

4 - Determine the sail's height, then fold it accordingly

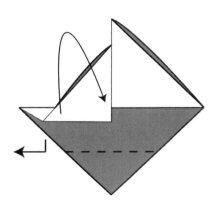

5 - Tuck the bottom edge inside the fold. Fold the bottom part to create a stand.

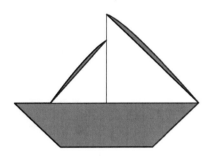

6 - Finish

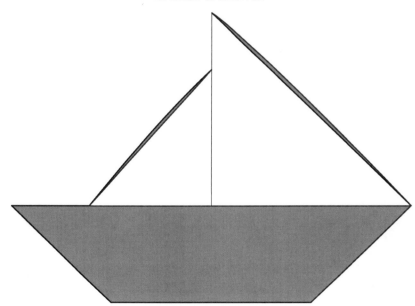

Urban

Pyramid

★ ☆ ☆

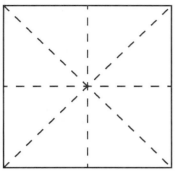

1 - Mark the folds

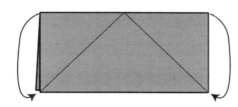

2 - Fold the four corners towards the centre of the paper

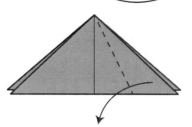

3 - Fold the peak along the crease

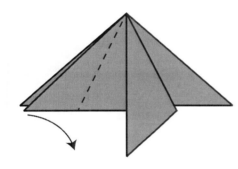

4 - Repeat with the second peak

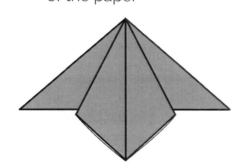

5 - Do the same with the opposite faces

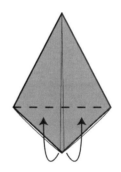

6 - Tuck the peaks inwards

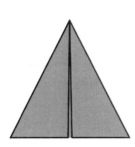

7 - Emboss

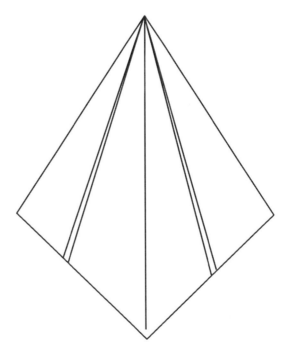

8 - You have constructed your pyramid

134

Hammerhead Plane

 ★ ★ ☆

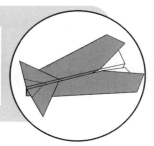

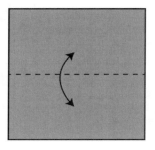

1 - Mark the fold in the center of the sheet.

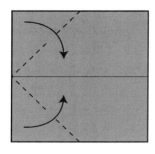

2 - Fold the corners towards the center, on the construction fold made in step 1.

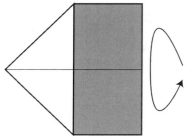

3 - Turn your origami over.

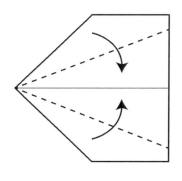

4 - Fold the ends again towards the center on the construction fold.

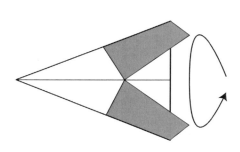

5 - Turn your origami over.

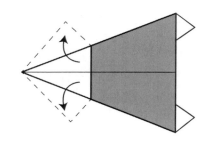

6 - Reopen the folds outward.

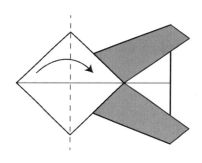

7 - Fold the square in half on the diagonal.

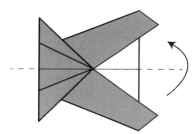

8 - Fold your origami in half lengthwise.

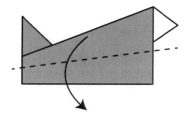

9 - Fold the wings to the side following the dotted lines.

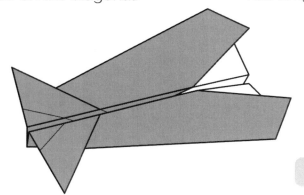

Your hammerhead plane is ready!

Fighter Plane

★ ★ ☆

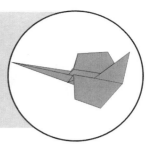

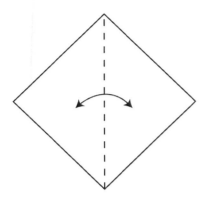

1 - Mark the fold in the middle of the sheet on the diagonal.

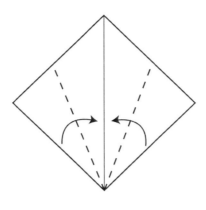

2 - Fold each part on the construction fold made in the previous step.

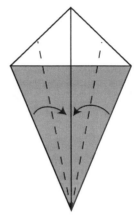

3 - Mark the fold on each side towards the center.

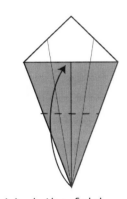

4 - Mark the fold.

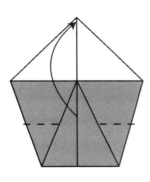

5 - Fold the bottom part following the dotted lines.

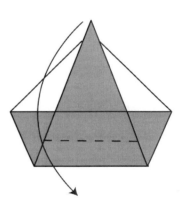

6 - Fold the tip downwards.

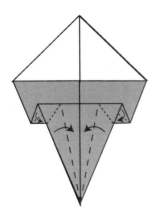

7 - Tuck in the corners of the bottom part following the construction fold made in step 3.

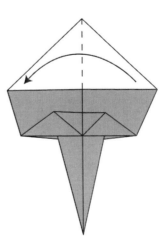

8 - Fold everything in half in the middle.

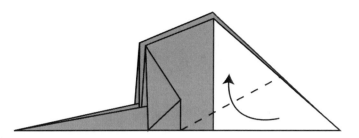

9 - Mark the fold of the rear part.

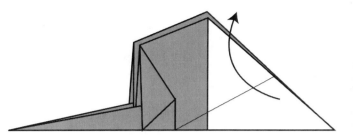

10 - Tuck the rear tip inside by reversing the fold.

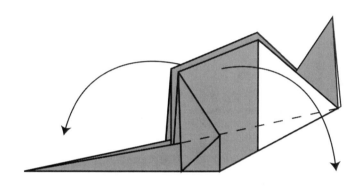

11 - Fold down the wings on each side.

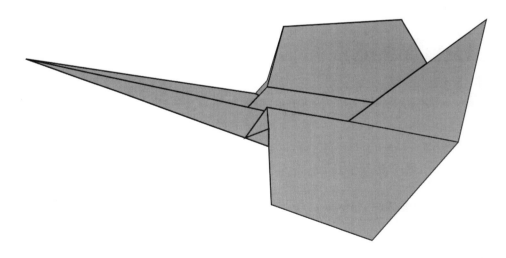

There you go, your fighter plane is ready to fly!

Ferry

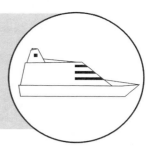

★ ★ ☆

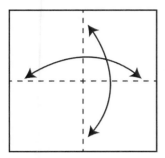

1 - Mark the folds following the dotted lines.

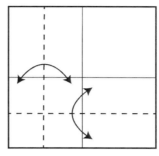

2 - Mark the folds by folding towards the center.

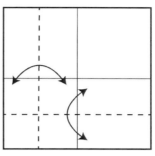

3 - Mark the folds following the dotted lines.

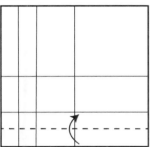

4 - Fold the end following the dotted lines.

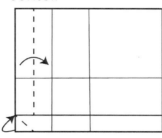

5 - Fold the end following the dotted lines, tuck the tip inside.

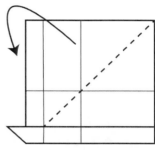

6 - Fold your origami in half.

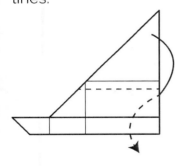

7 - Fold the tip downwards, tucking it inside.

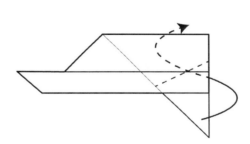

8 - Bring out the tip upwards.

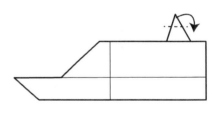

9 - Hide the tip inside.

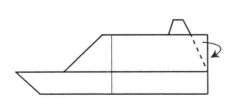

10 - Fold the corner inward.

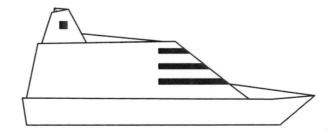

Your boat is ready!

Chip Cone

★ ☆ ☆

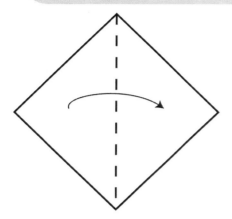

1 - Fold in half

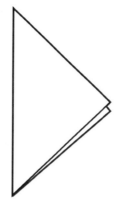

2 - Change direction

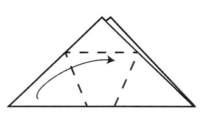

3 - Fold one peak
towards 2/3 of the
opposite side

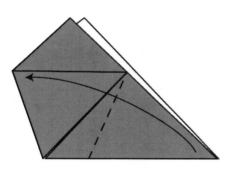

4 - Fold the tip towards
the opposite corner

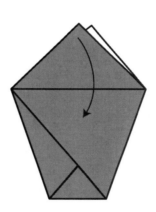

5 - Fold the tip
downwards

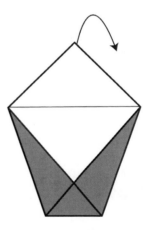

6 - Fold the triangle to
the other side

7 - Open up the inside
and your chip cone is
ready

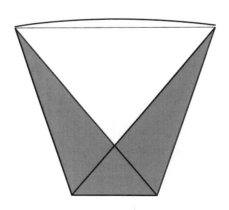

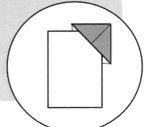

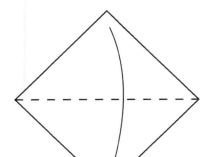

1 - Fold in half along the diagonal

2 - Mark the fold by connecting the sides to the tip

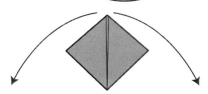

3 - Unfold

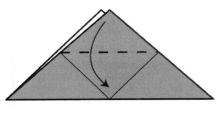

4 - Fold down the tip

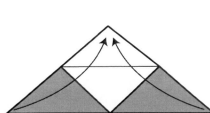

5 - Fold the corners upwards again

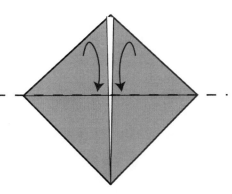

6 - Tuck the two tips inward by folding them

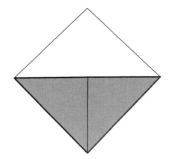
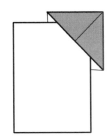

7 - Your bookmark is finished; all you have left to do is slip your bookmark onto the corner of your page

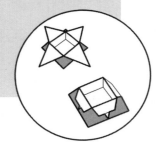

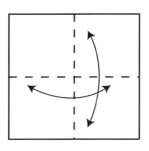

1 - Mark the folds following the dotted lines

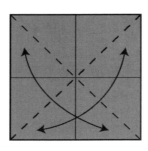

2 - Turn your origami over and mark the diagonal folds

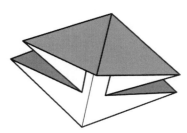

3 - Follow the direction of the construction folds and fold your origami

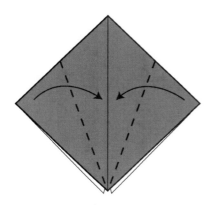

4 - With the opening facing downwards, fold the corners towards the centre

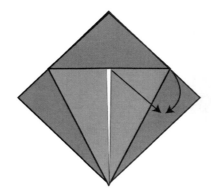

5 - Do the same with the opposite face

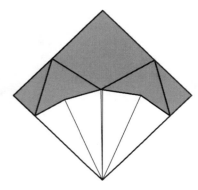

6 - Repeat with the other side

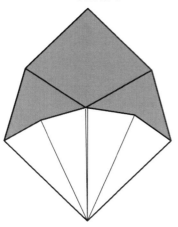

7 - Close these faces and open the sides

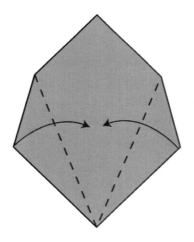

8 - Fold the edges for each side

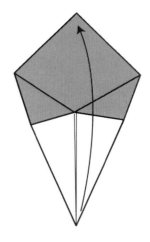

9 - Fold down the tip

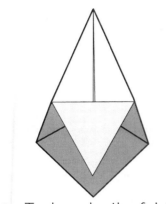

10 - Tuck under the folds

11 -Open and flatten the base

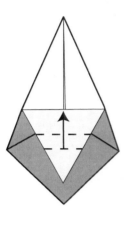

10 bis - Repeat for each side

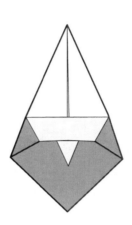

11 bis - Repeat for each face

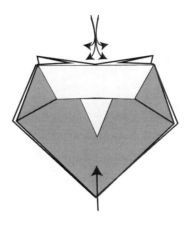

12 bis - Open and flatten the base

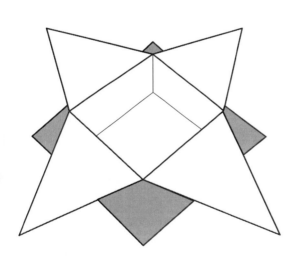

Version 1:
A pretty box with unfolded edges

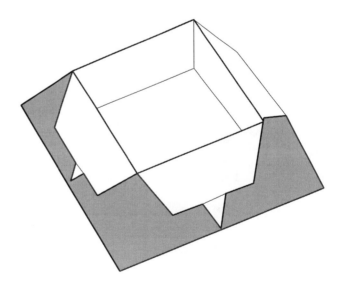

Version 2:
A pretty box with turned-up edges

Box

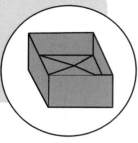

★ ★ ☆

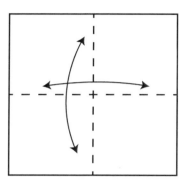

1 - Mark the folds

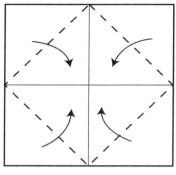

2 - Fold the four corners
towards the centre
of the sheet

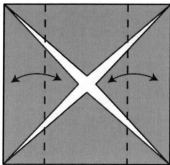

3 - Mark the folds again

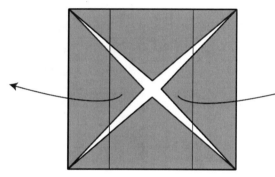

4 - Open the two
opposite corners

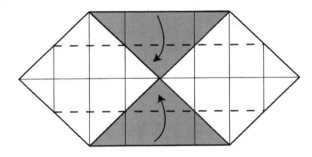

5 - Fold the ends towards the center

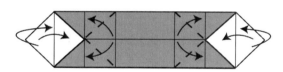

6 - Fold over the opposite corners
- Accentuate the box's shape
- Fold inwards

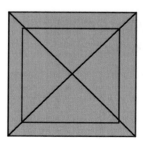

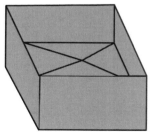

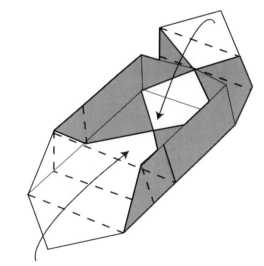

7 - Neatly fold the corners inward
Fold over the sides

There you have a lovely box

143

Envelope

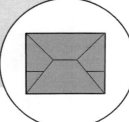

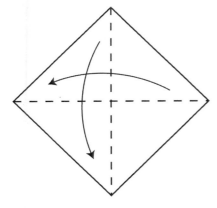

1 - Mark the diagonal folds

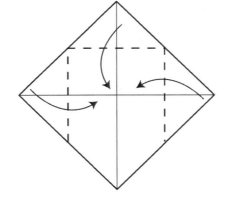

2 - Mark the folds of the 3 corners towards the centre

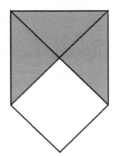

3 - Unfold

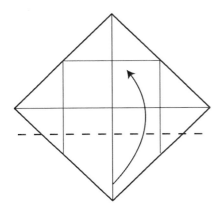

4 - Fold the 4th corner to the opposite fold line

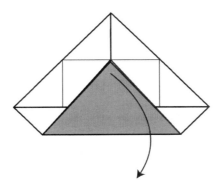

5 - Unfold

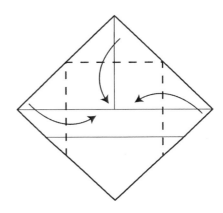

6 - Refold the 3 corners

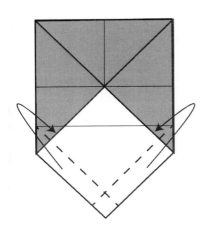

7 - Fold by folding over the opposite sides of the small triangles

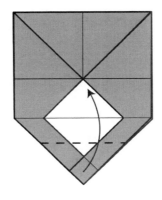

8 - Mark the fold by bending the tip towards the centre

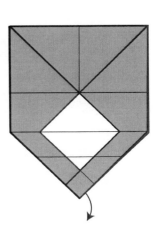

9 - Unfold the tip

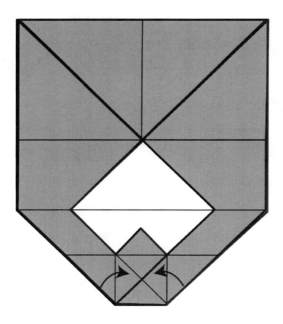

10 - Form a tip by folding the edges inward

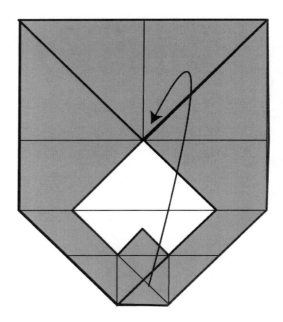

11 - Secure the side triangles using the tip by folding it inside the envelope

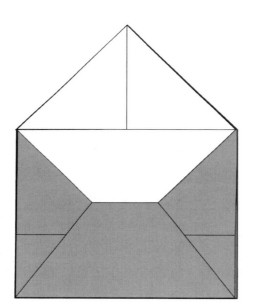

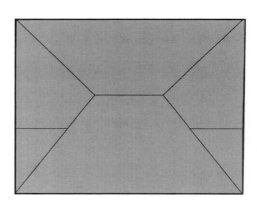

12 - Your envelope is complete

Fruit Basket

★ ★ ★

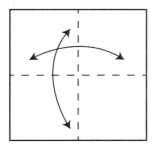

1 - Mark the folds by folding your sheet in half both ways.

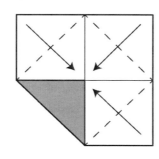

2 - Fold each corner towards the center.

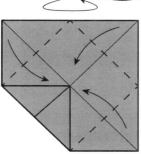

3 - Flip your origami over and refold each corner towards the center.

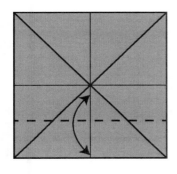

4 - Mark the fold by folding one side towards the center.

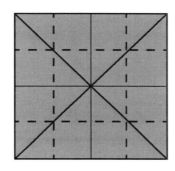

5 - Mark the folds in the same way on the other three sides.

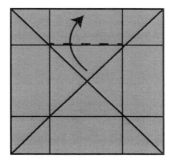

6 - Fold the center tips towards the edge, repeat on all corners.

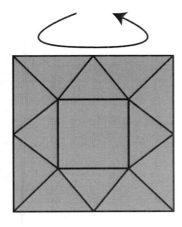

7 - Turn over your origami.

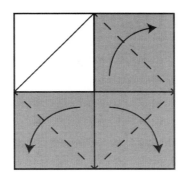

8 - Fold the center tips towards the outer corners.

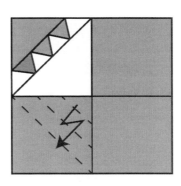

9 - Refold each corner accordion-style following the dotted lines.

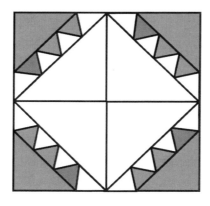

10 - Open your basket by pinching the corners.

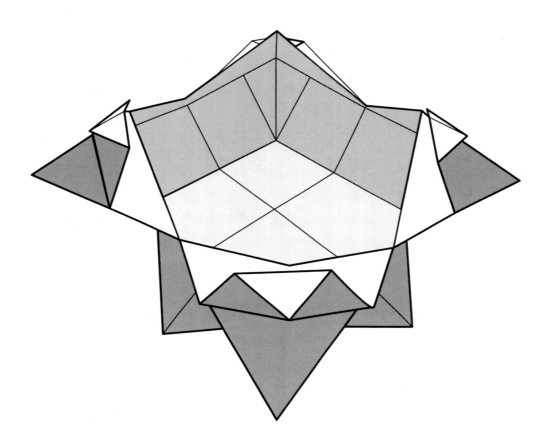

Your fruit basket is ready!

The Shirt

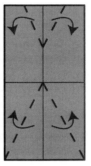

★ ☆ ☆

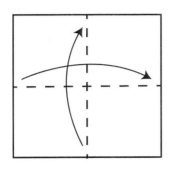

1 - Mark the folds.

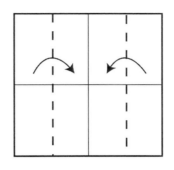

2 - Fold the ends towards the centre

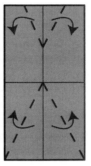

3 - Choose a collar width - Open and fold

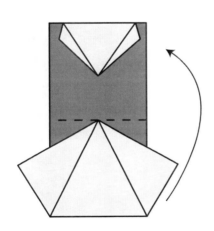

4 - Fold the lower par t to the back

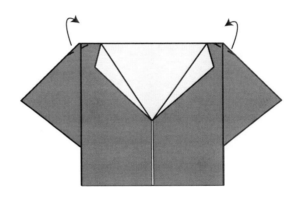

5 - You can emphasise the shoulders by folding them to the back

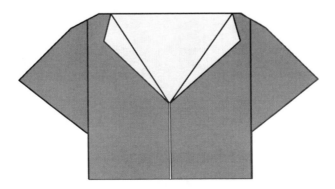

6 - End

148

Sweater

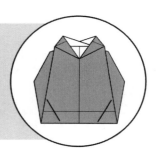

★ ☆ ☆

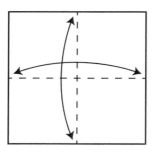

1 - Mark the folds in the center of the sheet.

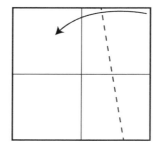

2 - Fold following the dotted lines.

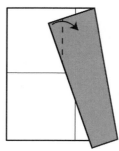

3 - Fold the corner following the dotted lines.

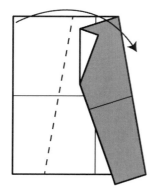

4 - Fold following the dotted lines.

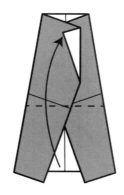

5 - Fold upwards following the dotted lines.

6 - Fold the corners following the dotted lines.

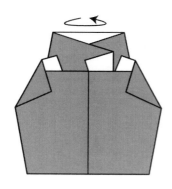

7 - Turn over your origami.

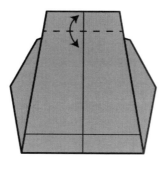

8 - Mark the fold.

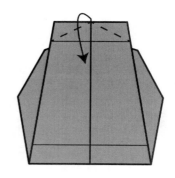

9 - Fold downwards.

Your sweater is ready!

Nightgown

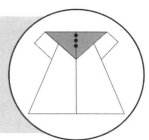

★ ☆ ☆

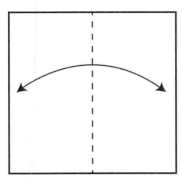

1 - Mark the fold in the center of the sheet.

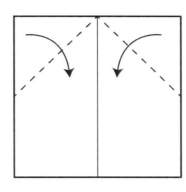

2 - Fold the corners towards the center.

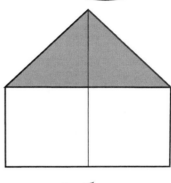

3 - Turn over your origami.

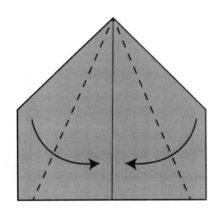

4 - Fold each end towards the center.

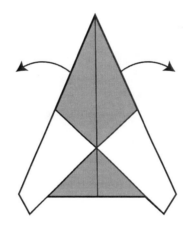

5 - Turn over your origami.

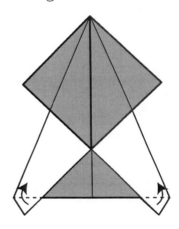

6 - Fold the corners upwards.

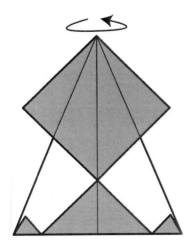

7 - Turn over your origami.

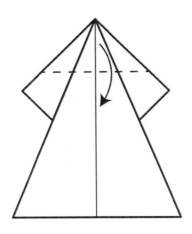

8 - Fold the upper corner downwards following the dotted lines.

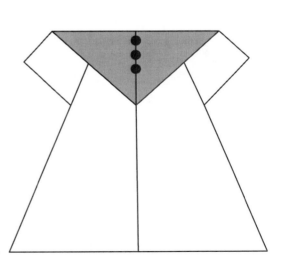

Draw the buttons and your dress is ready!

★ ☆ ☆

Dress

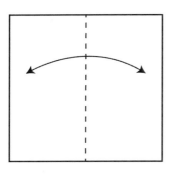

1 - Mark the fold in the center of the sheet vertically.

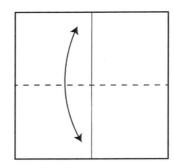

2 - Mark the fold in the center of the sheet horizontally.

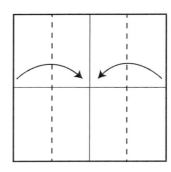

3 - Fold the ends towards the center.

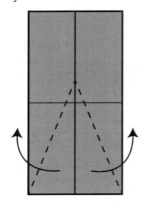

4 - Fold each lower corner outwards, diagonally by opening your origami.

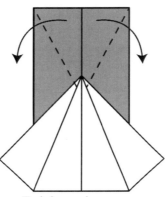

5 - Fold each upper corner outwards, diagonally by opening your origami.

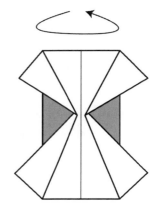

6 - Turn over your origami.

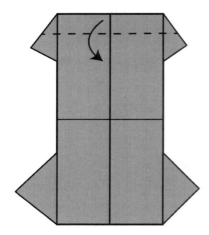

7 - Fold the top downwards following the dotted lines.

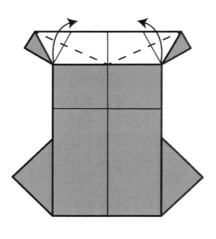

8 - Fold the corners upwards to create the collars.

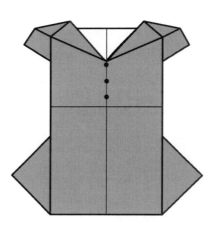

Your dress is ready!

Clothing
Evening Dress

★ ☆ ☆

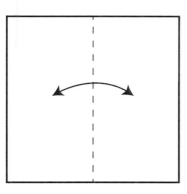

1 - Mark the fold in the middle.

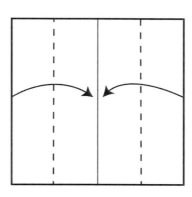

2 - Fold each side towards the center.

3 - Fold the two corners to form the collar.

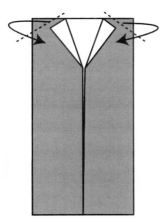

4 - Fold the ends backwards.

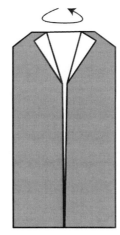

5 - Turn over your origami.

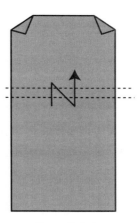

6 - Accordion fold your origami slightly above the center.

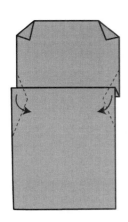

7 - Fold the corners into a triangle.

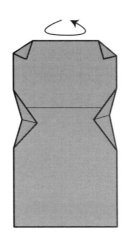

8 - Turn over your origami.

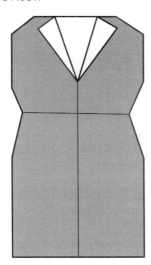

Your dress is ready!

T-shirt

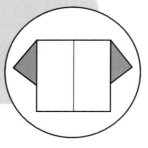

★ ☆ ☆

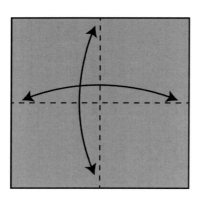

1 - Mark the folds following the dotted lines.

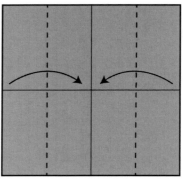

2 - Fold each end towards the center.

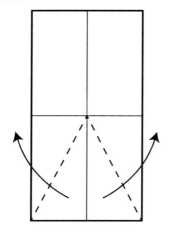

3 - Unfold the two corners outwardly.

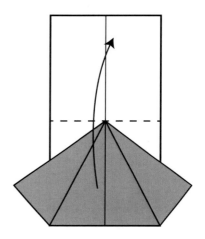

4 - Fold your origami in half.

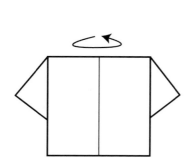

5 - Turn over your origami.

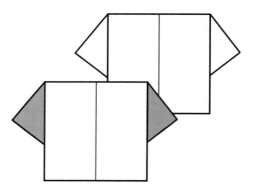

Your T-shirt is ready!

Clothing
Summer Dress
★ ★ ☆

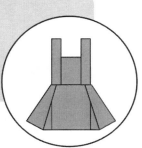

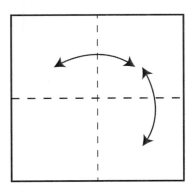

1 - Mark the folds.

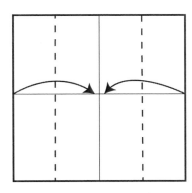

2 - Fold each side towards the center.

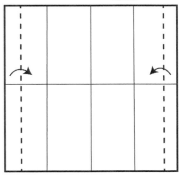

3 - Fold the two corners, following the dotted lines.

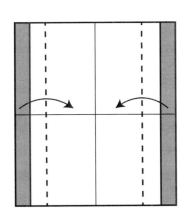

4 - Fold the ends towards the center, to the back.

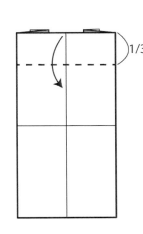

5 - Fold down the top part, opening the fold.

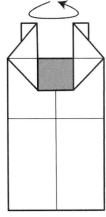

6 - Turn over your origami.

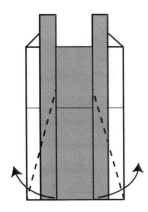

7 - Fold the corners into triangles outwardly.

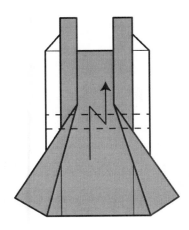

8 - Accordion fold in the middle.

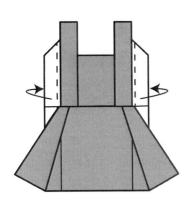

9 - Fold the corners inward.

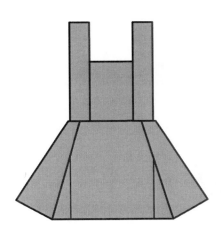

Your dress is ready!

Made in United States
North Haven, CT
05 December 2023

45077251R10087